Claudette Hudelson

Scenes from My Window

Notes from the Publisher

Composers In Focus is a series of original piano collections celebrating the creative artistry of contemporary composers. It is through the work of these composers that the piano teaching repertoire is enlarged and enhanced.

It is my hope that students, teachers, and all others who experience this music will be enriched and inspired.

Frank J. Hackinson

Frank J. Hackinson, Publisher

Notes from the Composer

One of my dear piano teacher friends is always coming up with ideas for me for composition titles. One day she said, "I want you to write a collection of pieces with titles of things you see when you look out of your bay window. You could call it 'Scenes from My Window'." As I thought about it, there were many different things that came to my attention. I thought of the titles first, then it was easy for me to come up with a musical idea that fit the title. It was even more fun coming up with the teacher accompaniments. I wrote the words last of all.

I hope you enjoy playing the music in this collection as much as I did writing it.

Musically yours,

Claudette Hudelson

Claudette Hudelson

Contents

Wind in the Trees

Claudette Hudelson

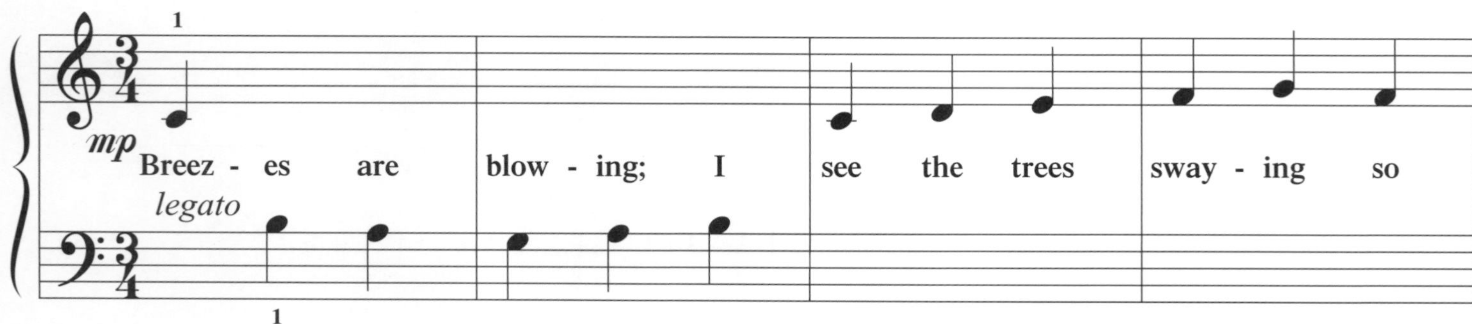

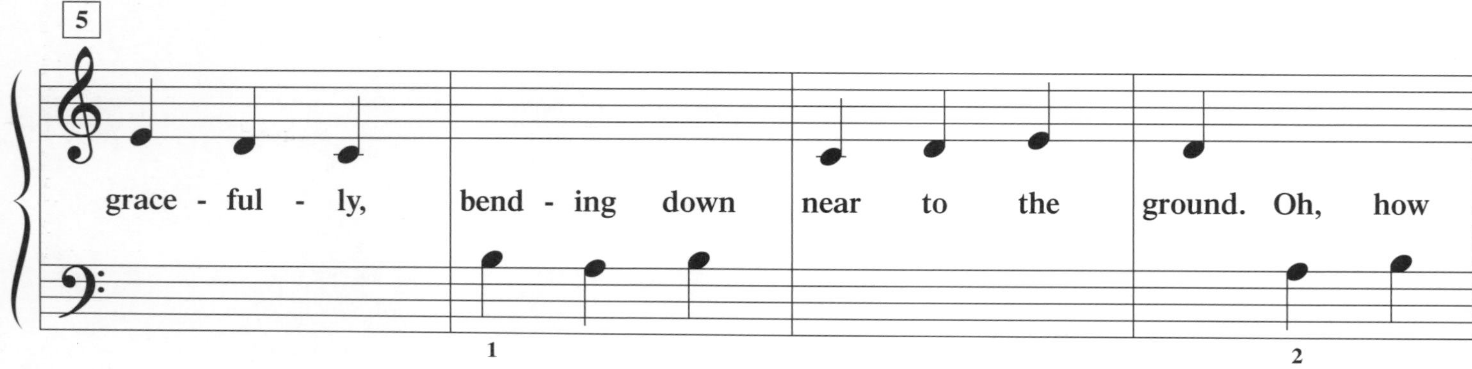

Teacher Duet: (Student plays 1 octave higher)

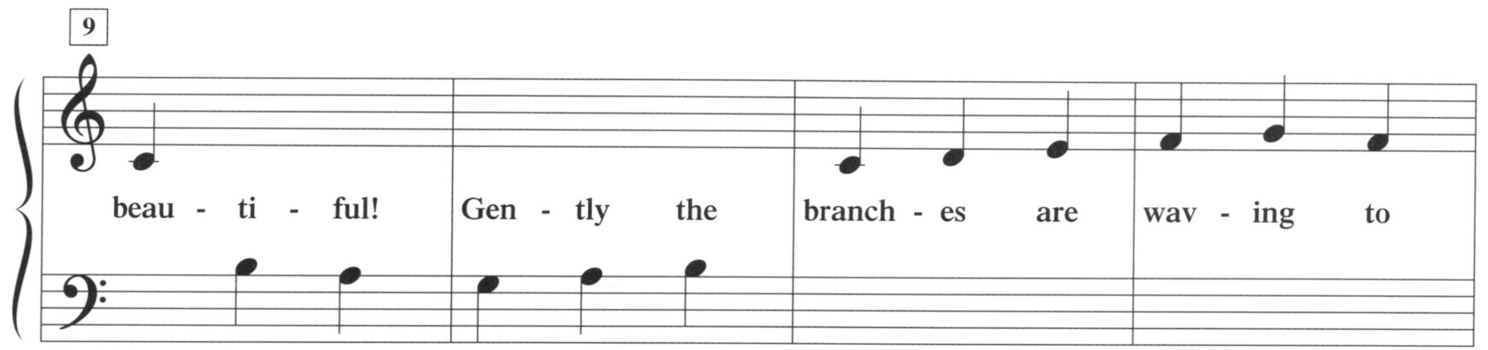
9
beau - ti - ful! Gen - tly the branch - es are wav - ing to

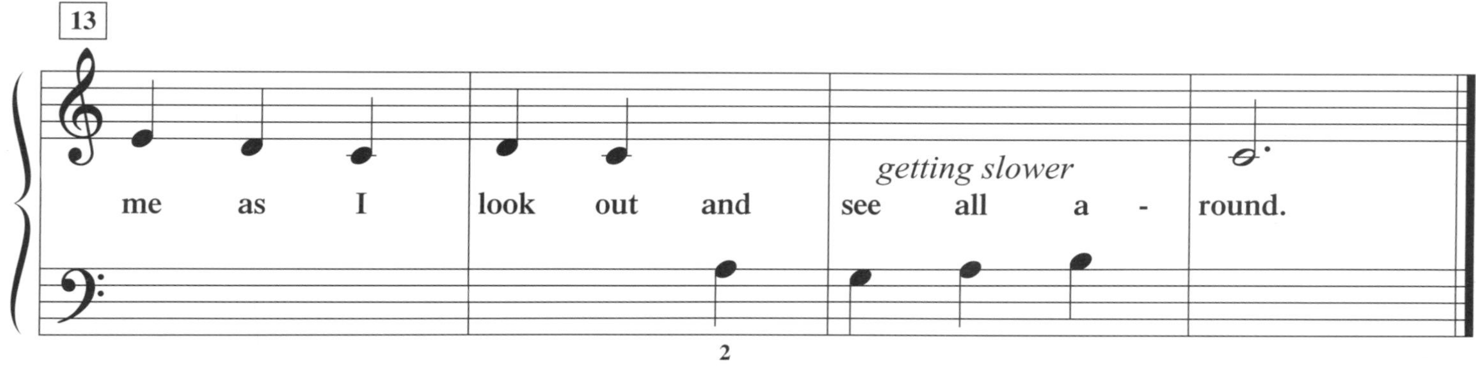
13
me as I look out and see all a - round.
getting slower
2

9
5
2
1
13
rit.

Children Playing

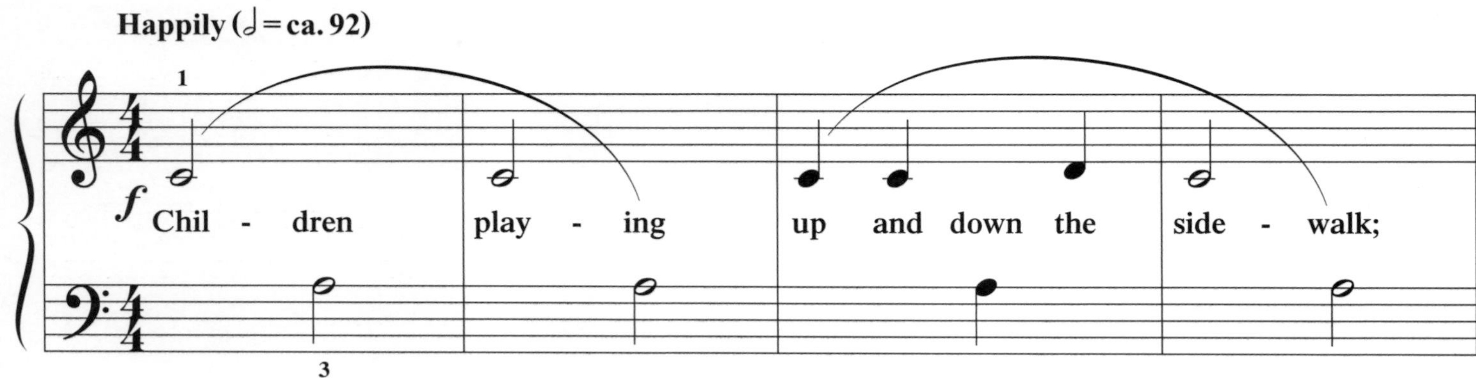

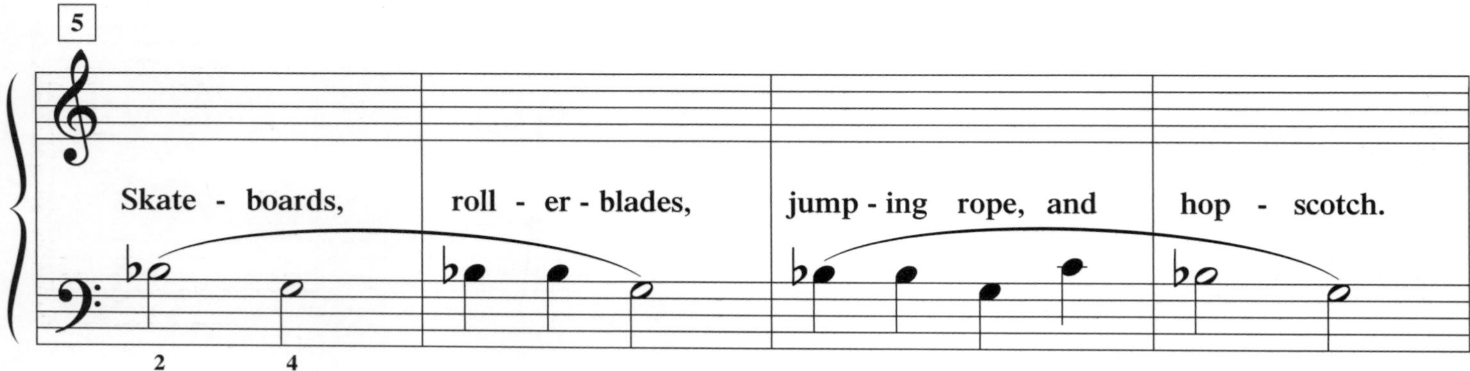

Teacher Duet: (Student plays 1 octave higher)

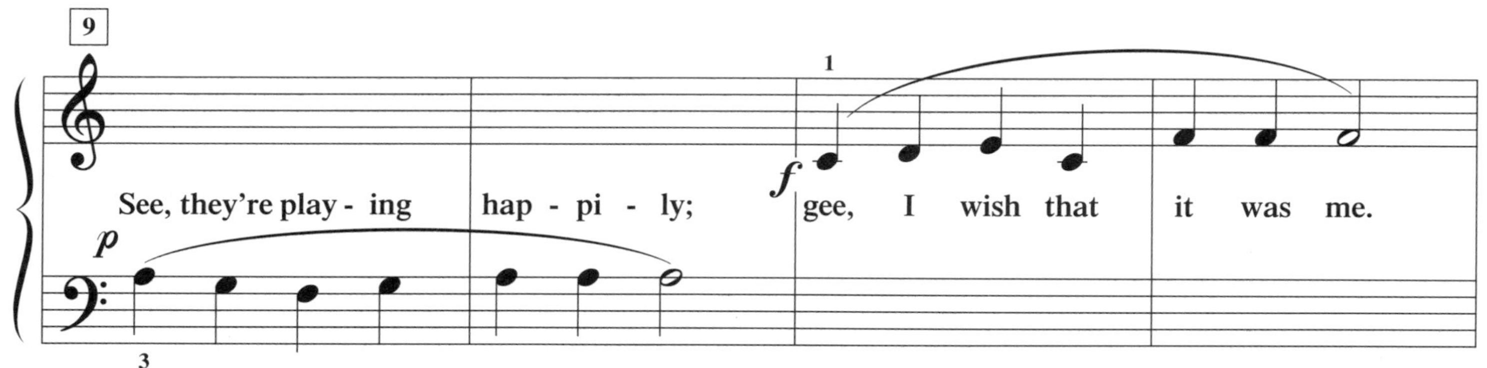
9
1
See, they're play - ing
hap - pi - ly;
gee, I wish that
it was me.
p
f
3

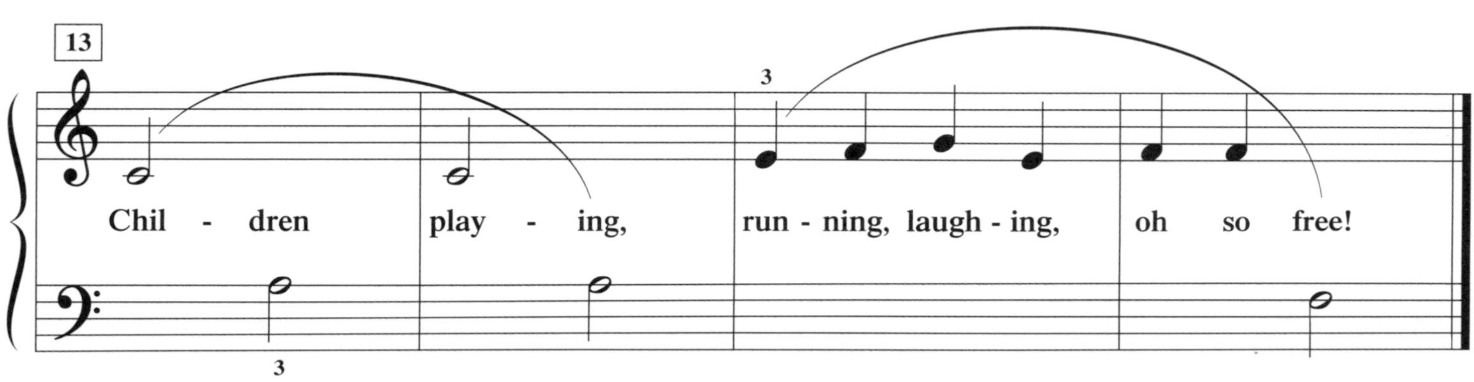
13
3
Chil - dren
play - ing,
run - ning, laugh - ing,
oh so free!
3

9
pp
mf
13

Kids Following the Leader

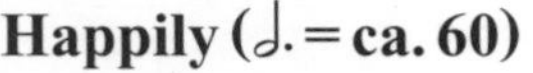

1
f Fol - low the lead - er and do what I do, as we're
1

5
2
hop - ping and skip - ping, and jump - ing a - long.
2

9
1
p Is - n't it fun to do all that the lead - er does,
1

13
2
f sing - ing a song as we skip a - long?
2

Teacher Duet: (Student plays 1 octave higher)

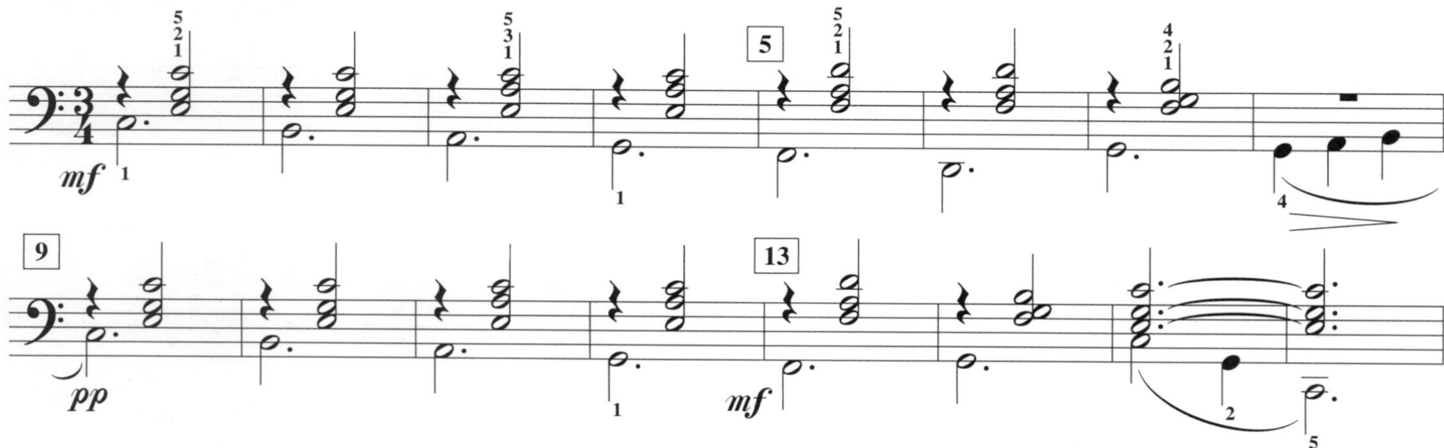

17
Down the street, 'cross the yard, up the steps, off the porch;
p
21
See, can you do what I'm try - ing to do?
25
I'm look - ing back to see if you are be - hind me.
f
29
It's so much fun to be lead - er, too!
17
pp
21
25
mf
29

The First Jonquil's Bloom

Beautifully (♩ = ca. 120)

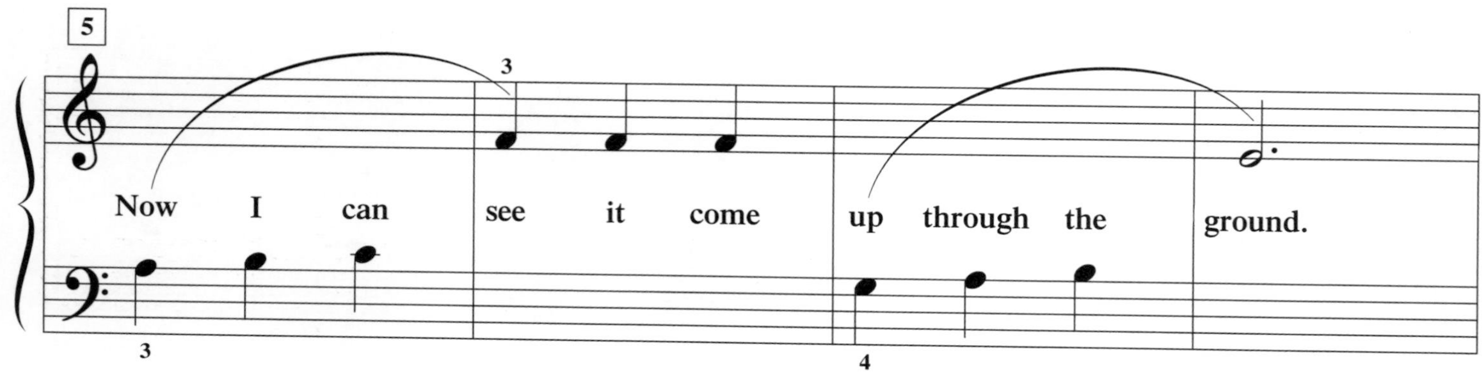

Teacher Duet: (Student plays 1 octave higher)

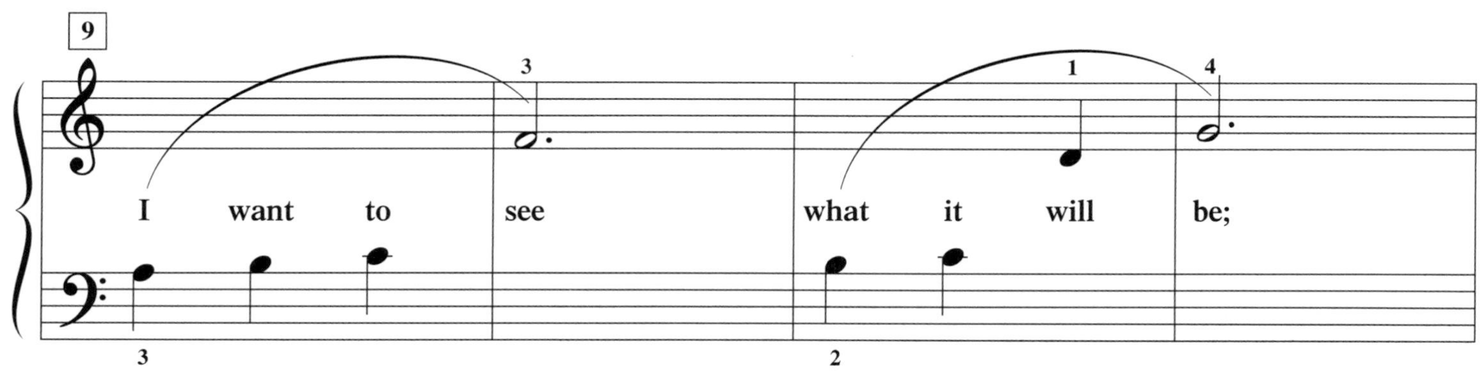
9
3
1
4
I want to see
what it will
be;
3
2

13
3
4
2
getting slower
p
Yel - low or
cream, it's
pret -
ty.
mf
3
2
1

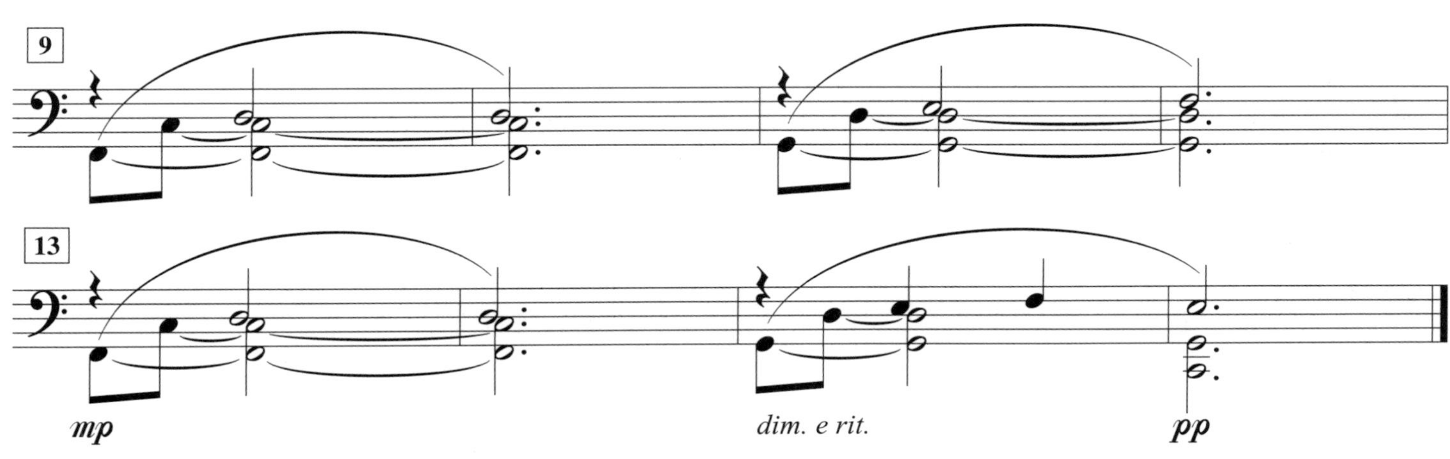
9
13
mp
dim. e rit.
pp

Raindrops Falling

Gently (♩= ca. 132)

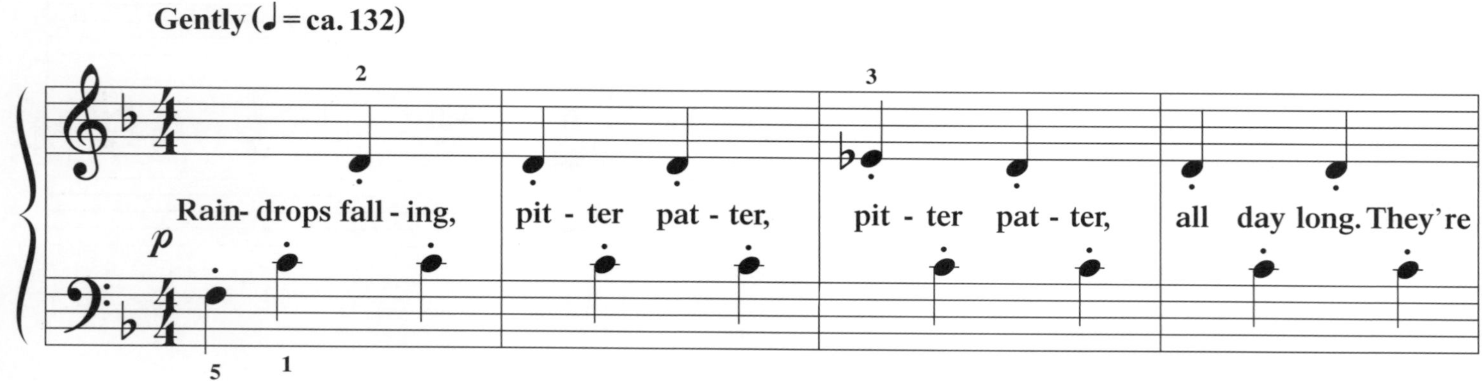

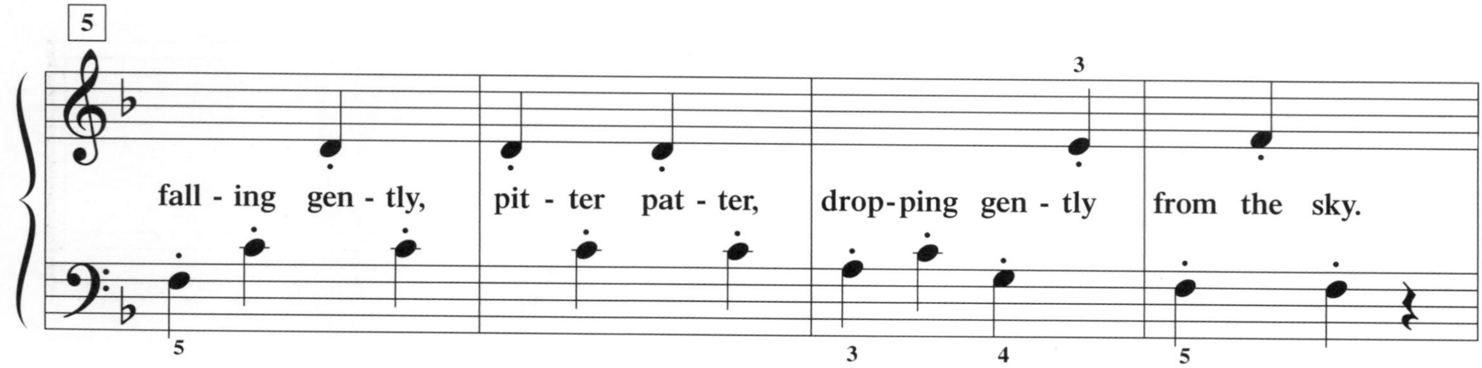

Teacher Duet: (Student plays 1 octave higher)

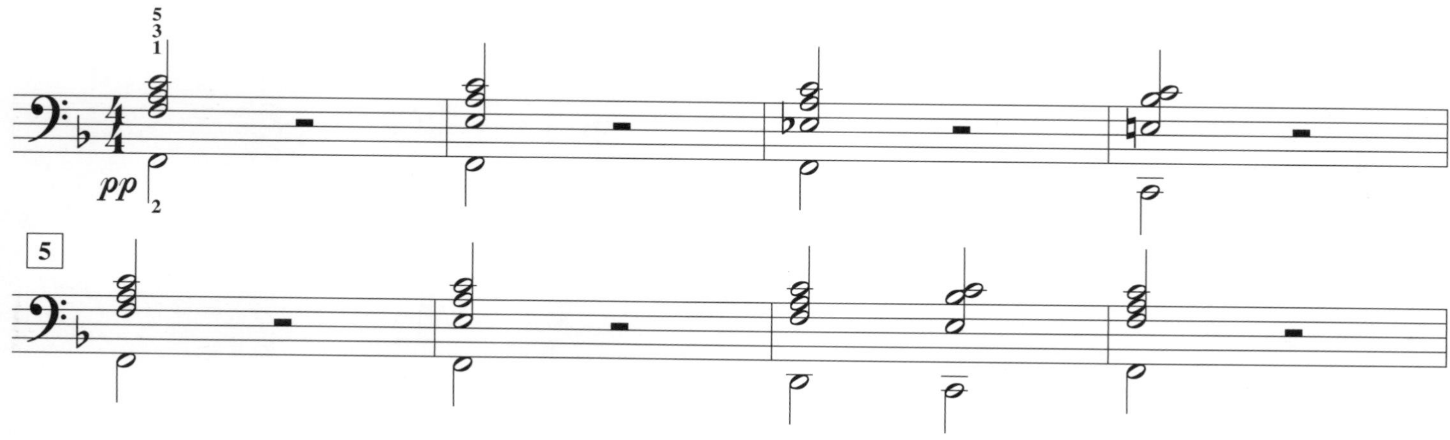

9
4
2
f
See them glis - ten,
spark - ling, shin - ing,
drop - ping down a - mong the tree - tops.
1

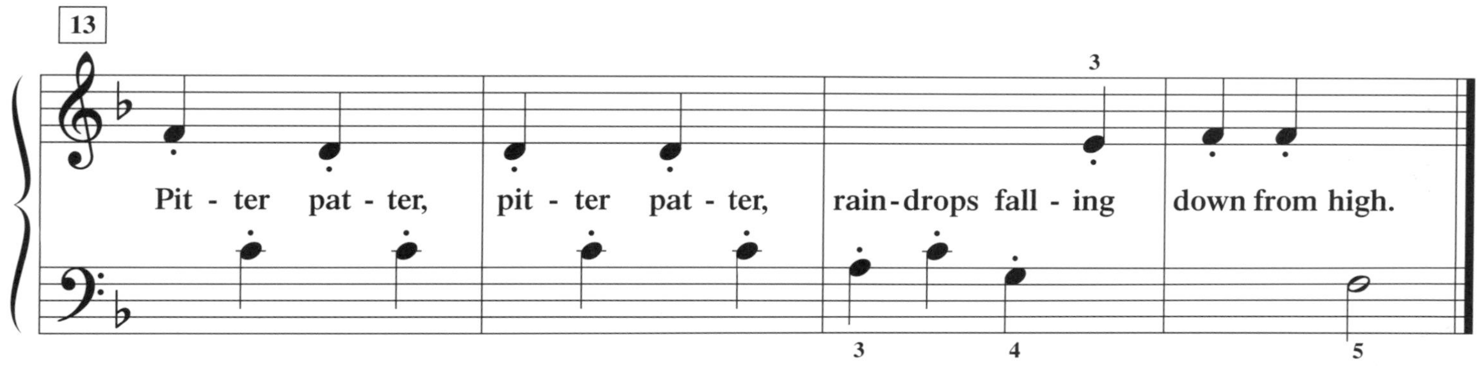
13
3
Pit - ter pat - ter,
pit - ter pat - ter,
rain - drops fall - ing
down from high.
3
4
5

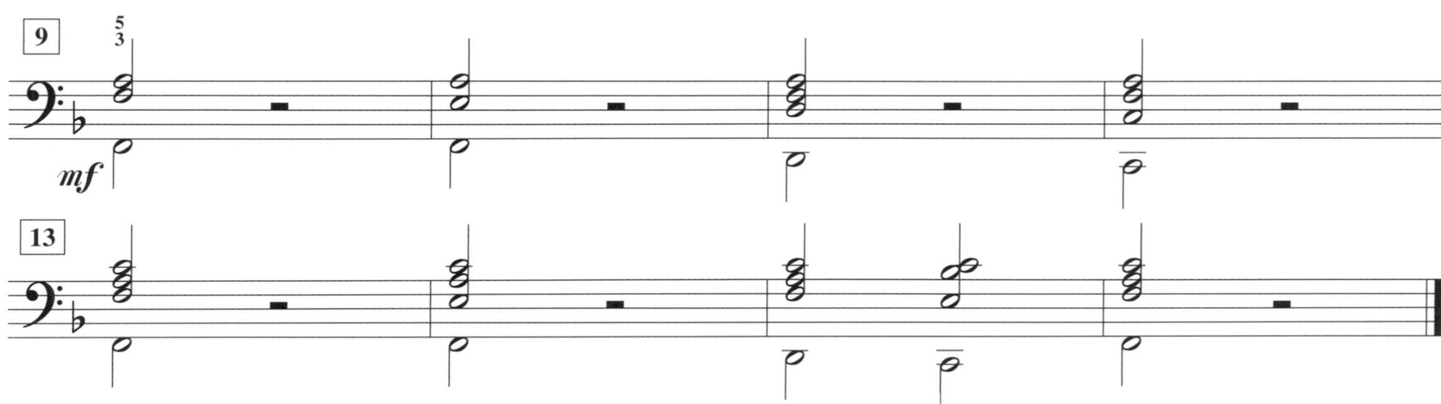
9
5
3
mf
13

Baby Robins in a Nest

Moderately (♩= ca. 132)

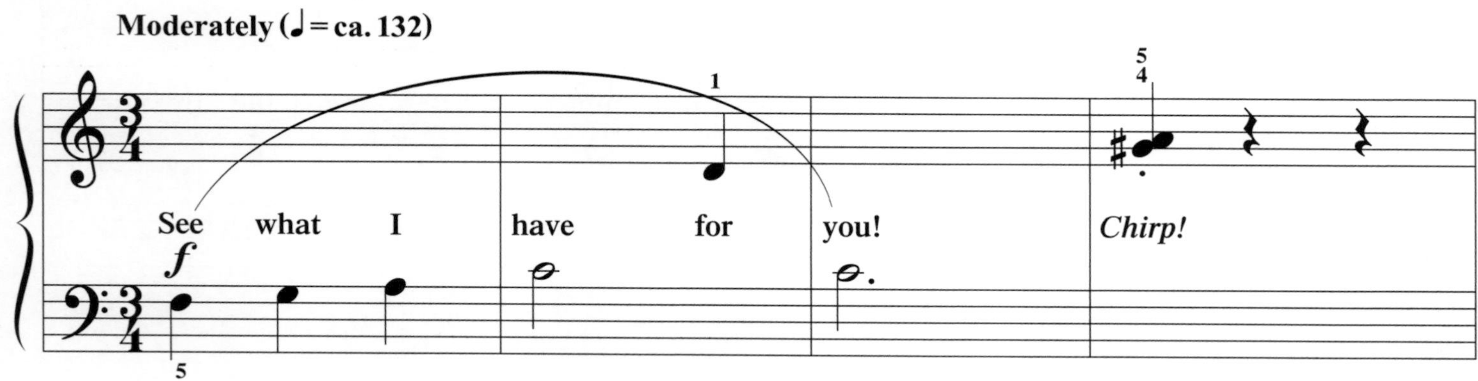

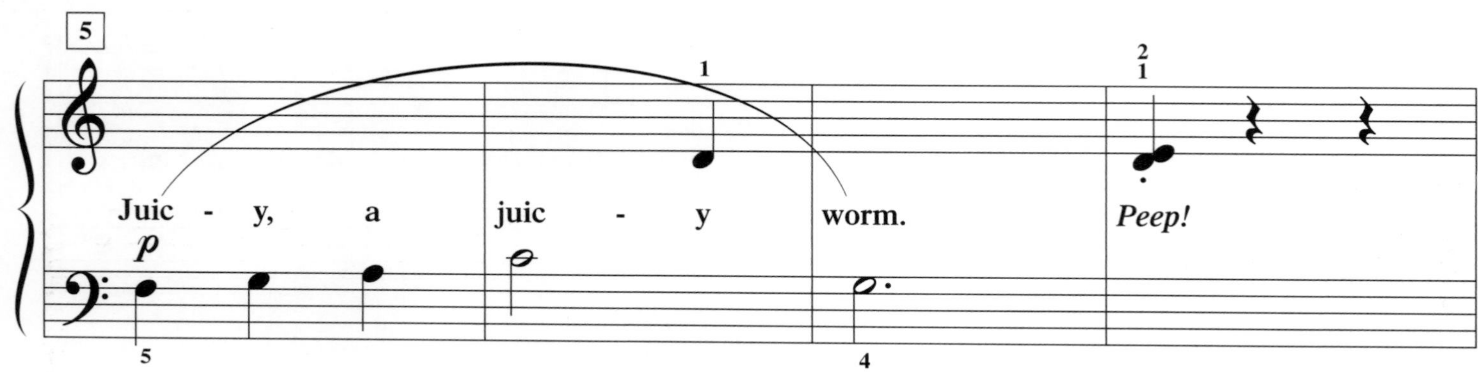

Teacher Duet: (Student plays 1 octave higher)

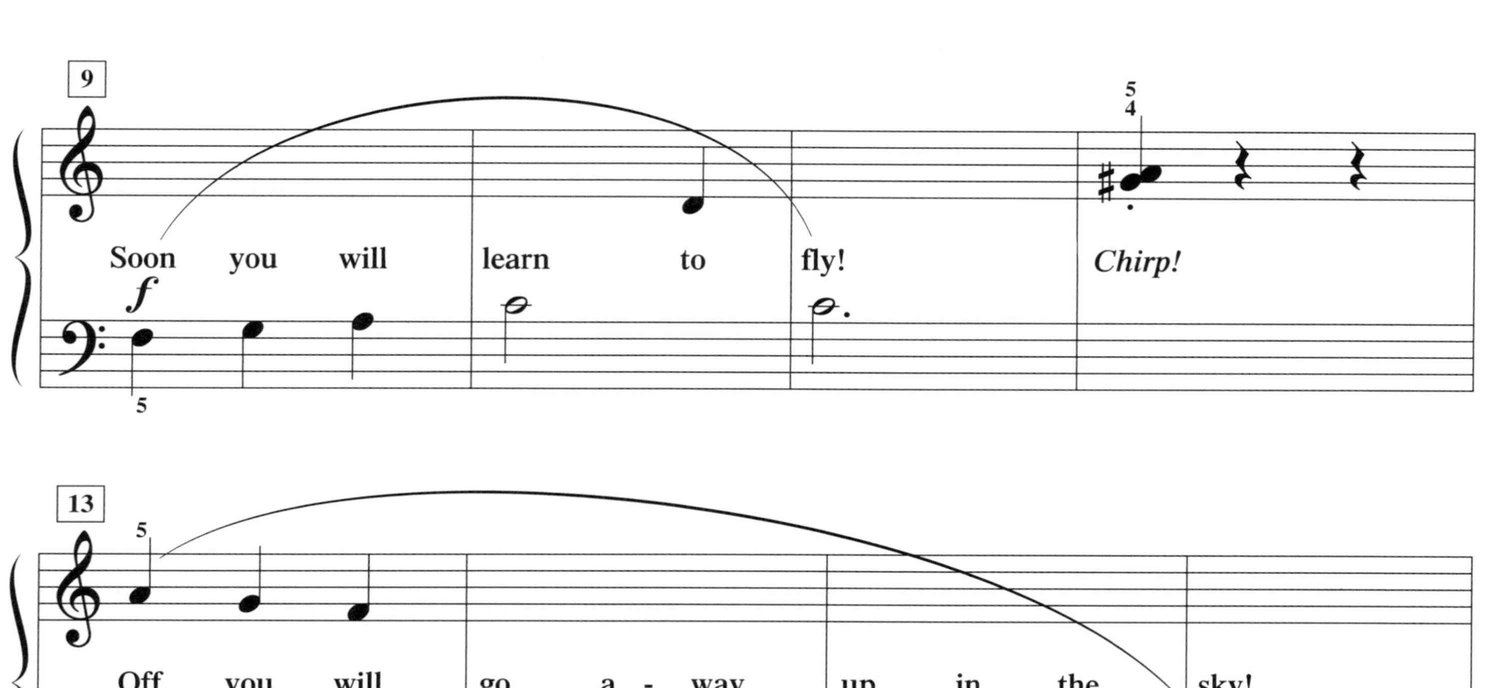
9
Soon you will learn to fly!
Chirp!
13
Off you will go, a - way up in the sky!

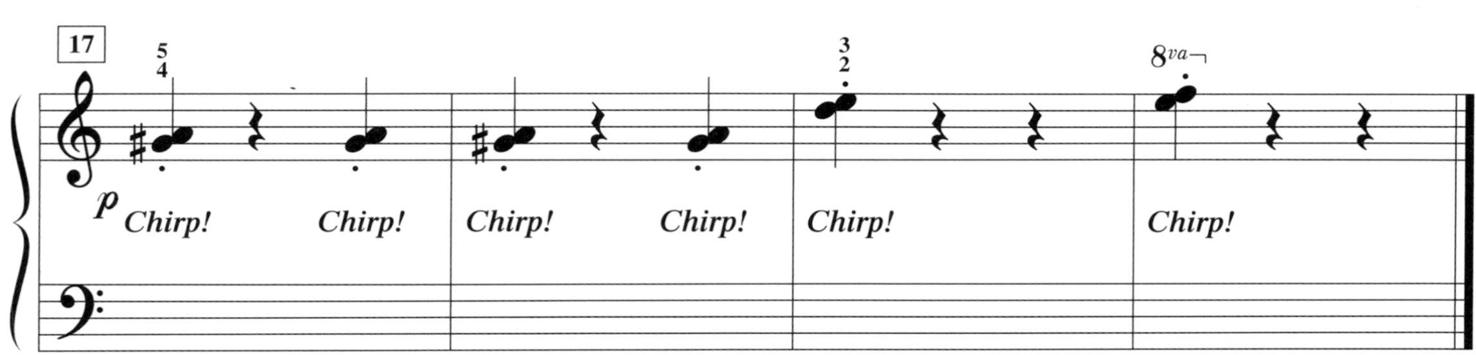
17
Chirp! Chirp! Chirp! Chirp! Chirp! Chirp!

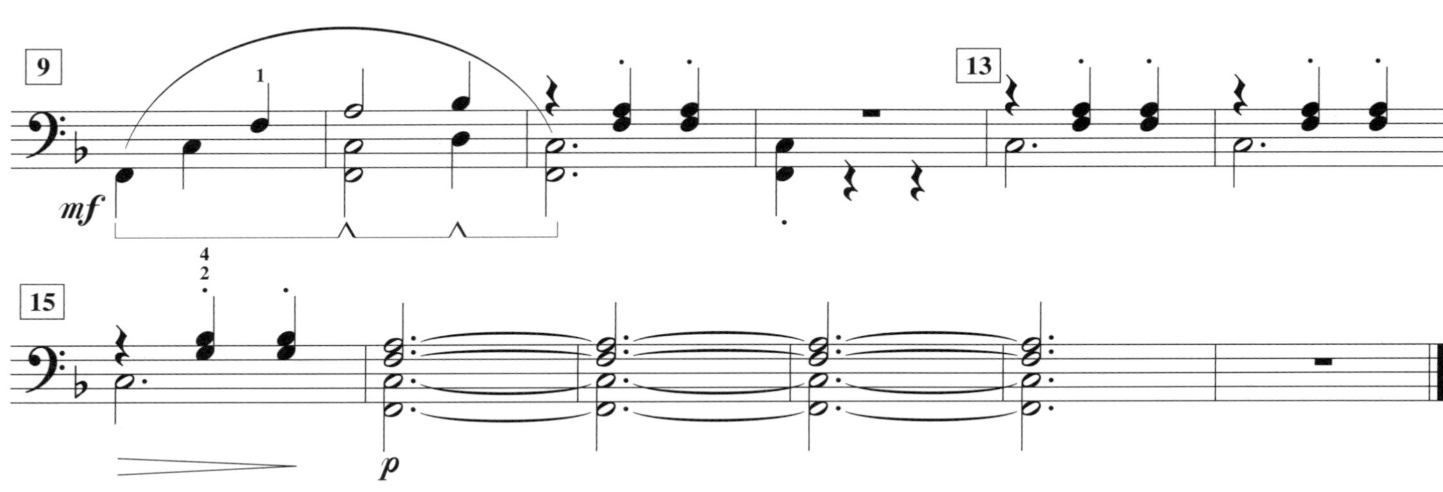

My Pretty Flowers

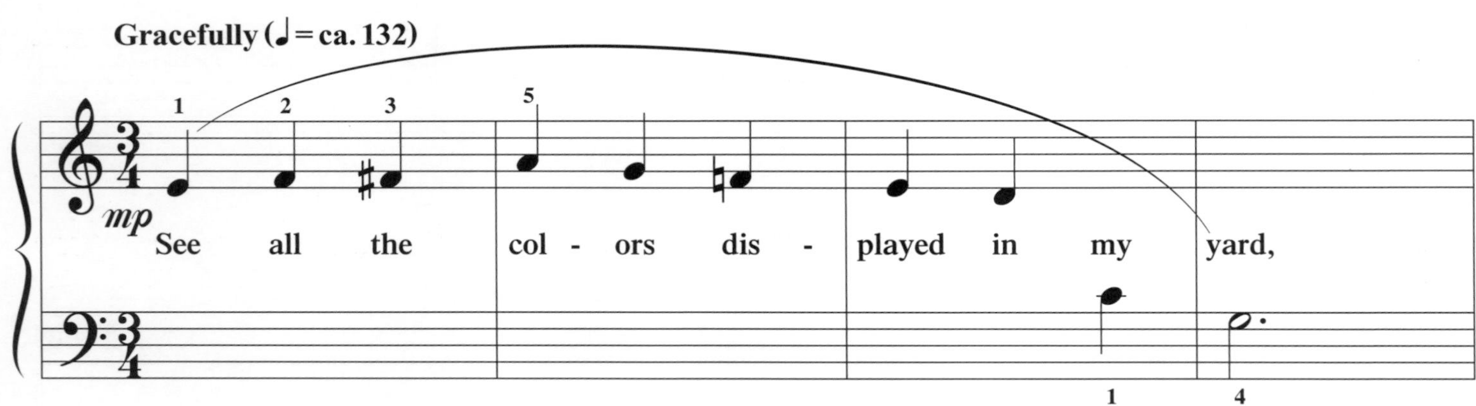

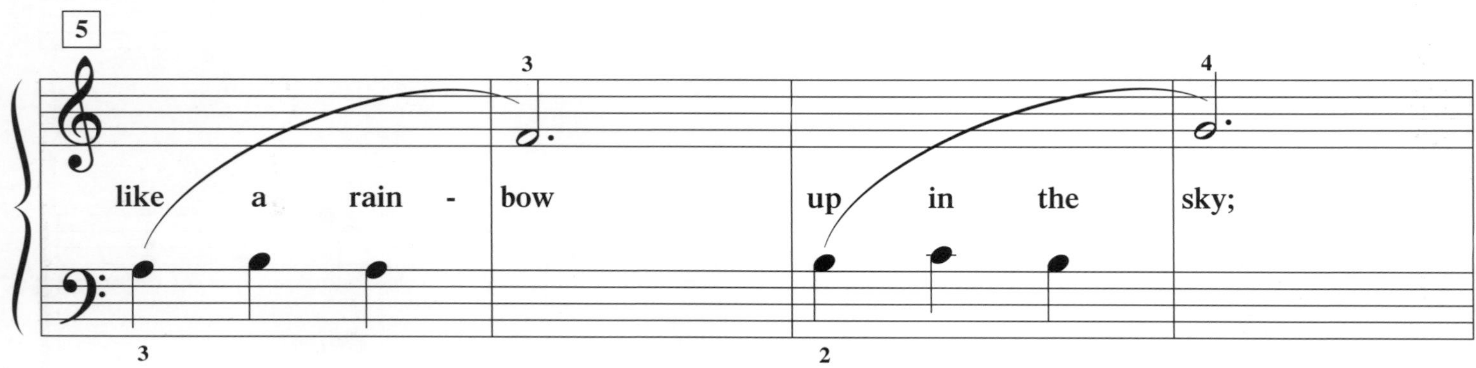

Teacher Duet: (Student plays 1 octave higher, without pedal)

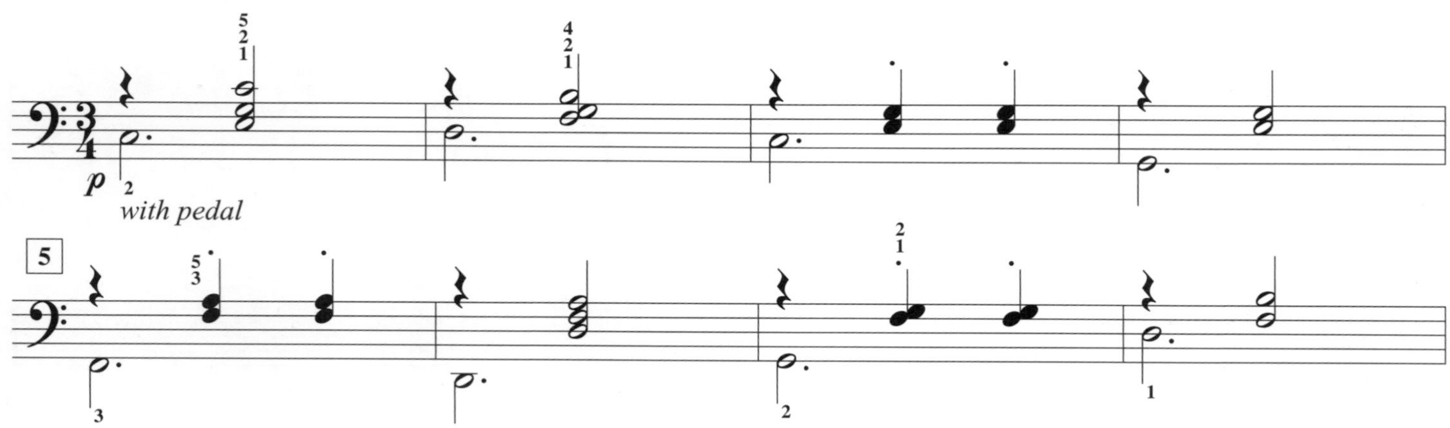

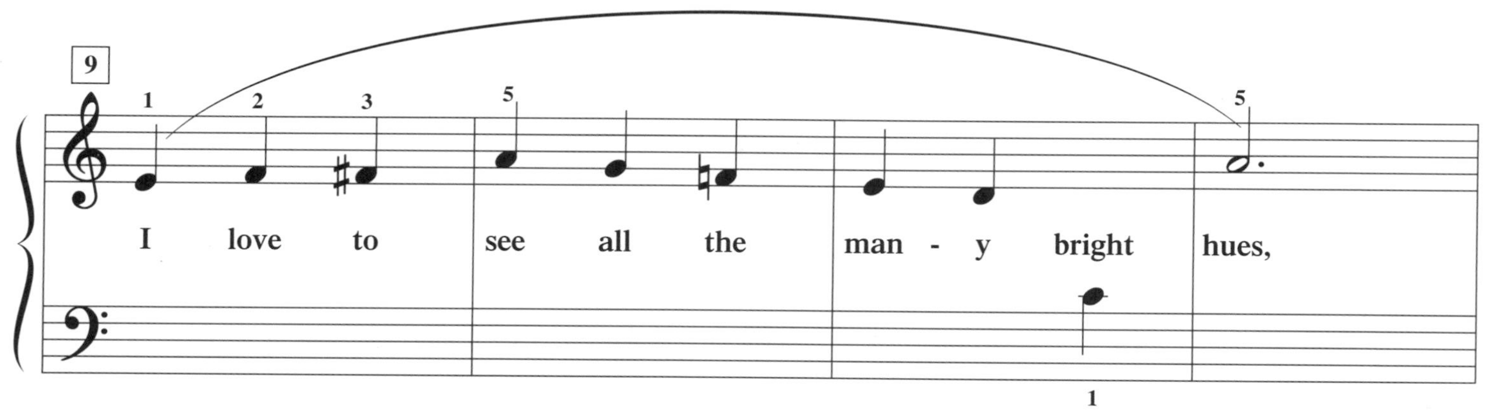
9
I love to see all the man - y bright hues,

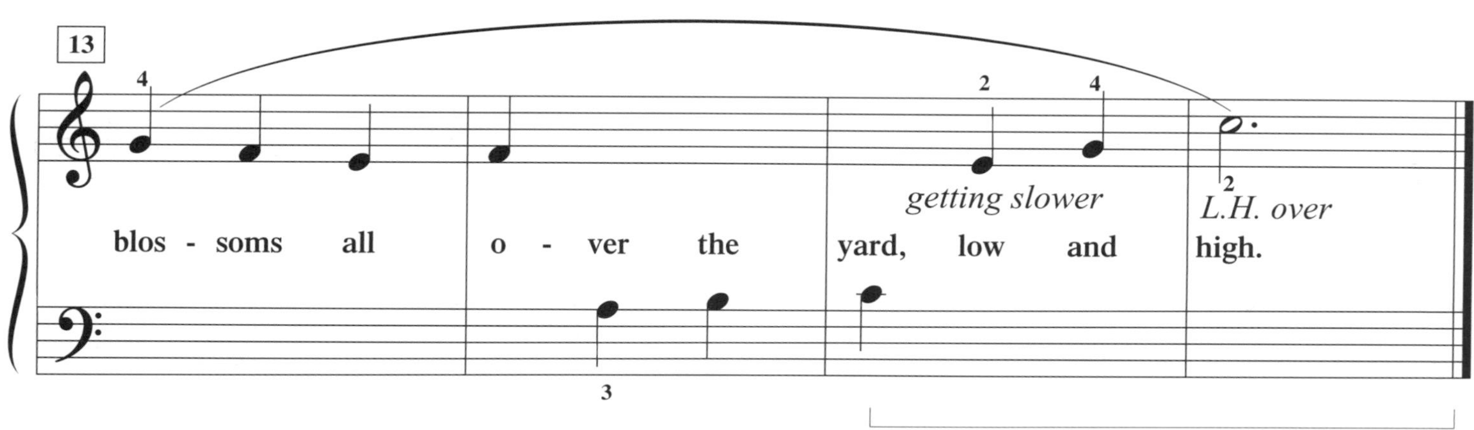
13
blos - soms all o - ver the yard, low and high.
getting slower
L.H. over

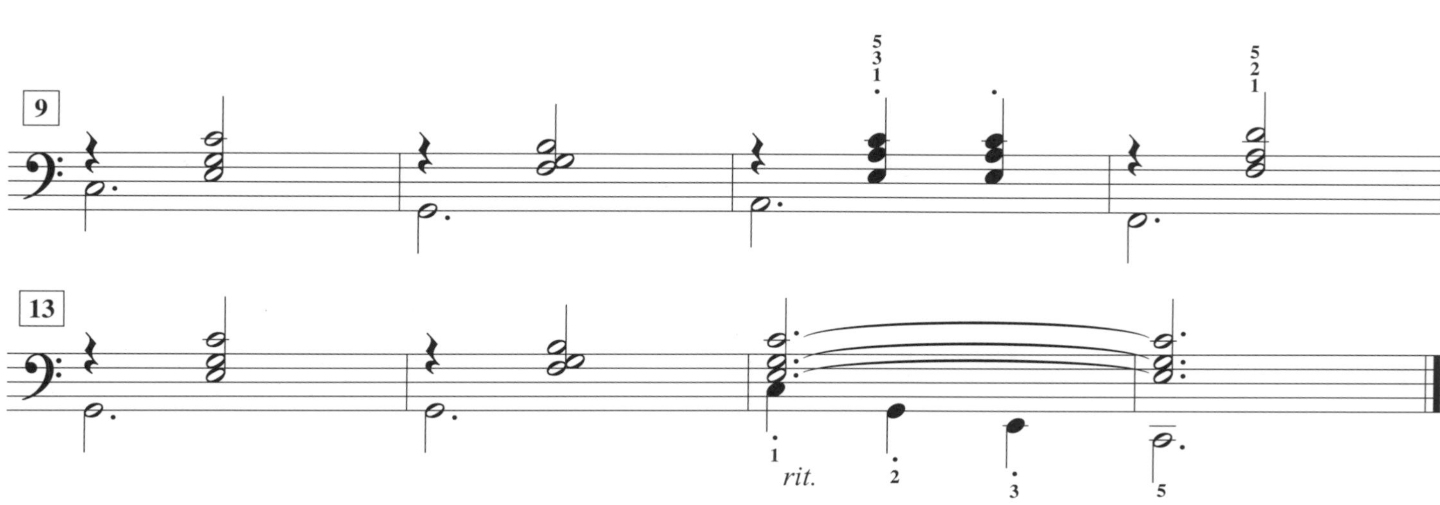
9
13
rit.

Walking the Dog

Read steps + skips (not finger numbers)

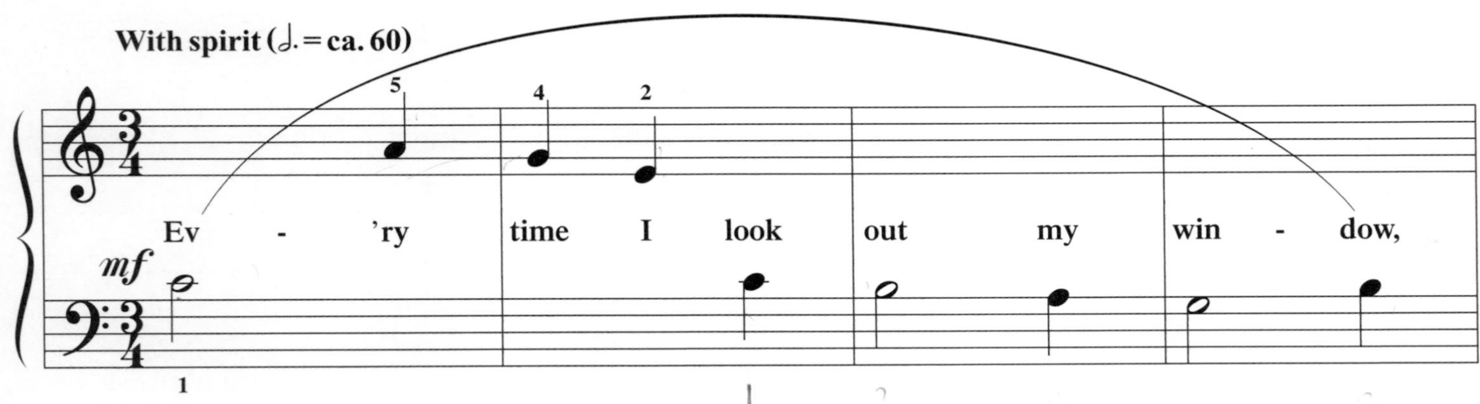

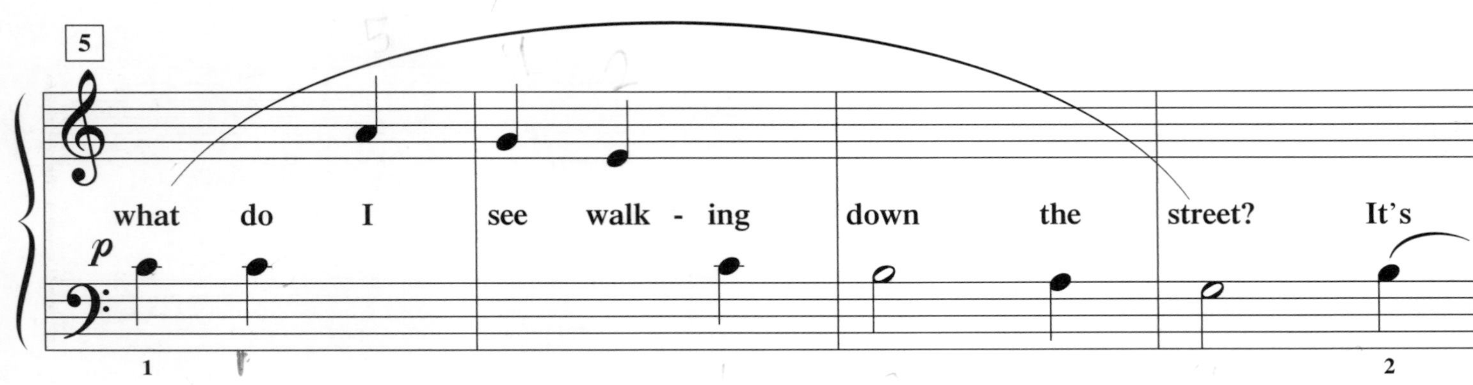

Teacher Duet: (Student plays 1 octave higher, without pedal)

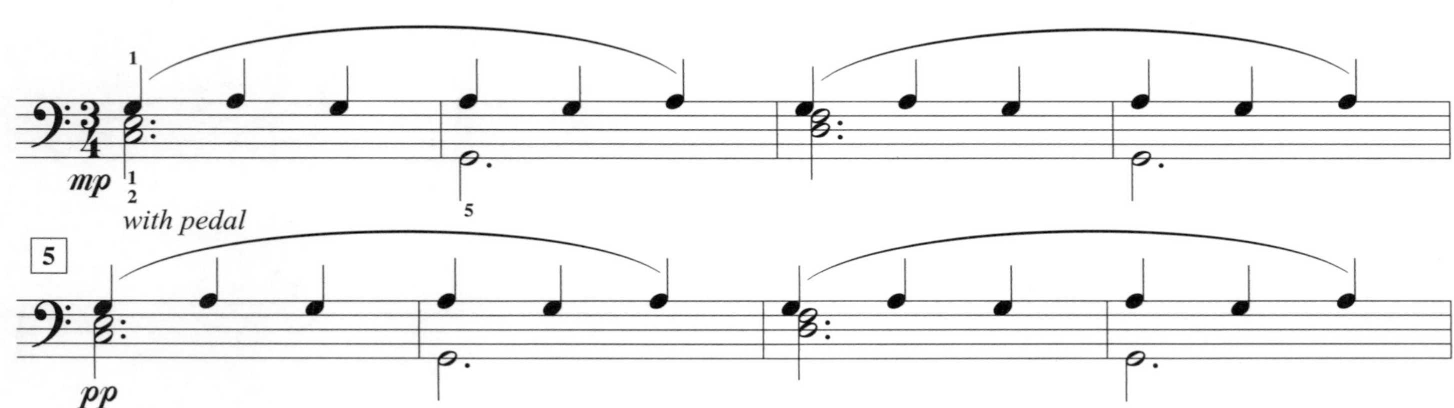

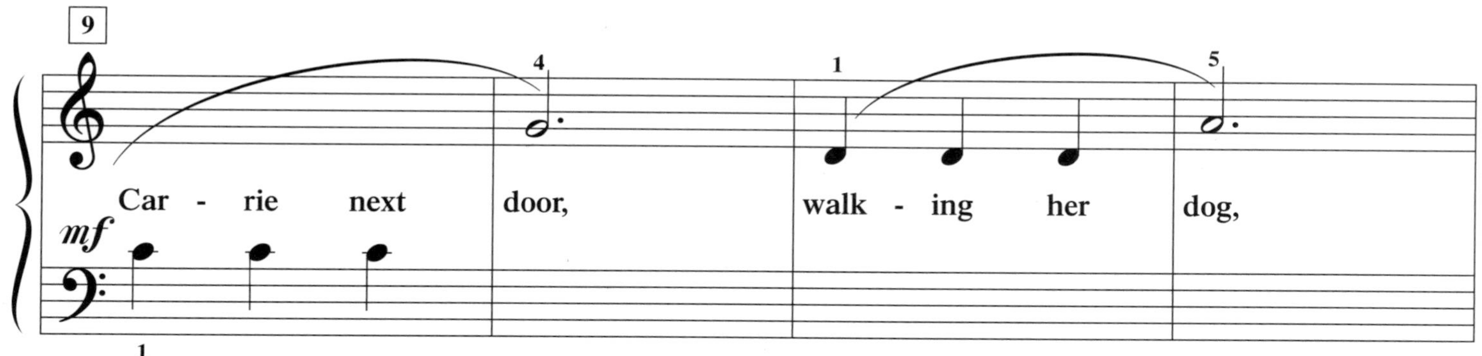
9
4
1
5
Car - rie next door, walk - ing her dog,
mf
1

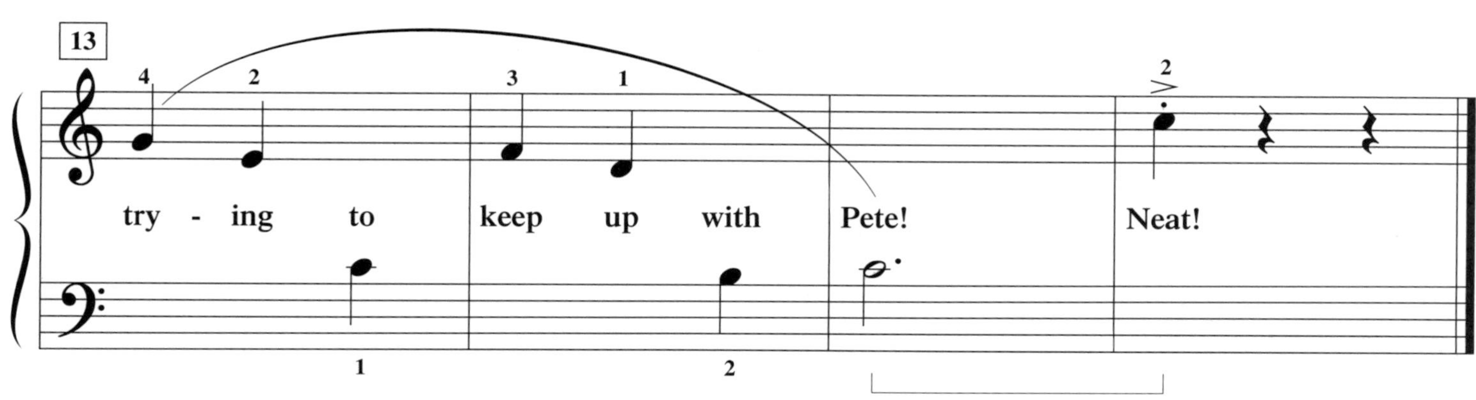
13
4
2
3
1
2
try - ing to keep up with Pete! Neat!
1
2

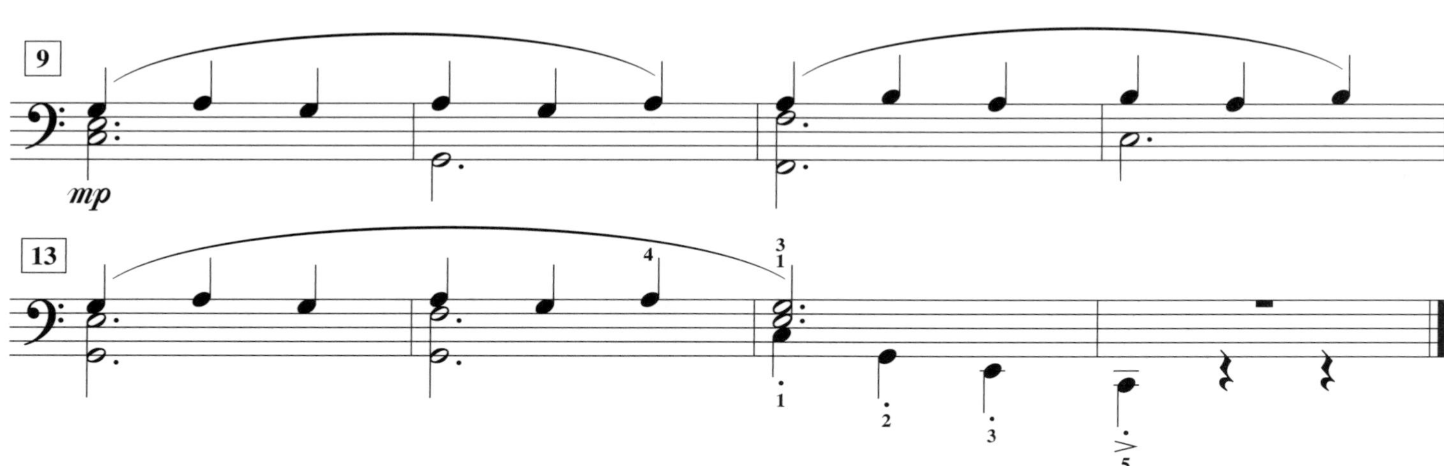
9
mp
13
4
3
1
1
2
3
5

Grasshopper Parade

Jumpily (♩ = ca. 132)

Teacher Duet: (Student plays 1 octave higher)

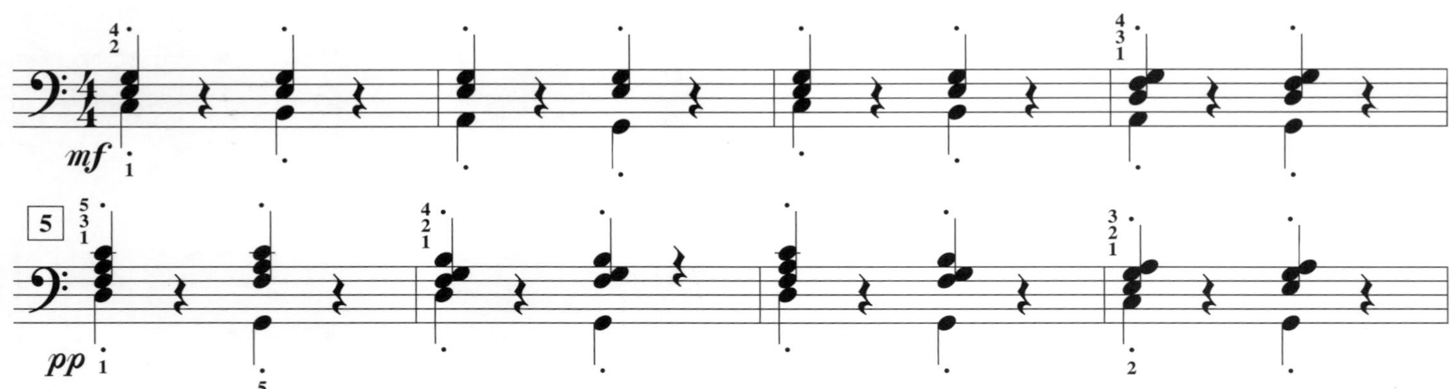

9
2
4
5
4
f

13
3
4
2
3
4

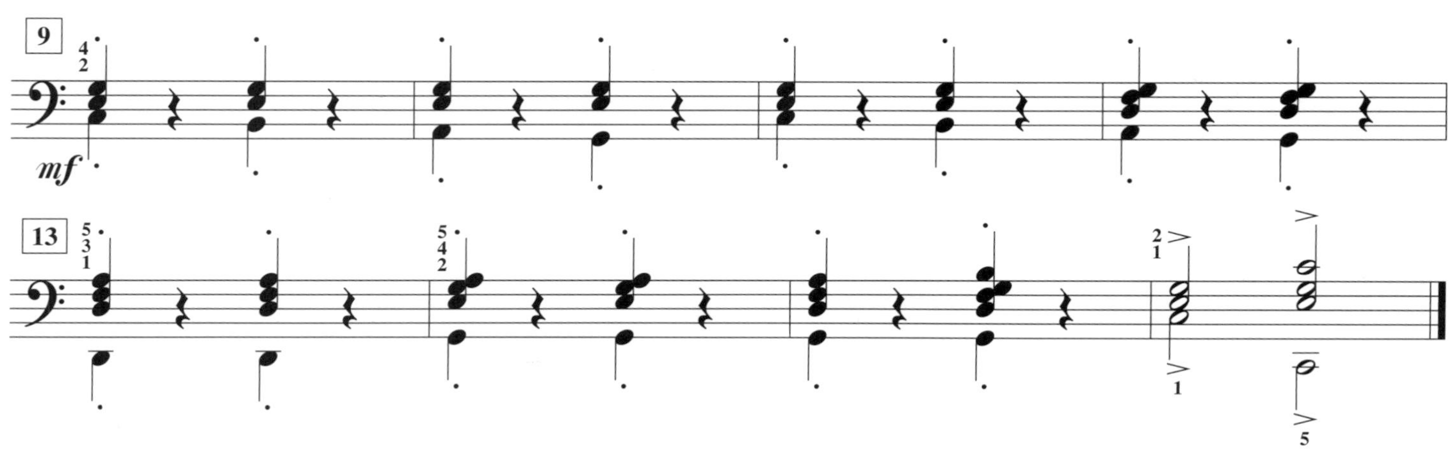
9
4
2
mf
13
5
3
1
5
4
2
2
1
1
5

My White Picket Fence

Waltz tempo (♩ = ca. 144)

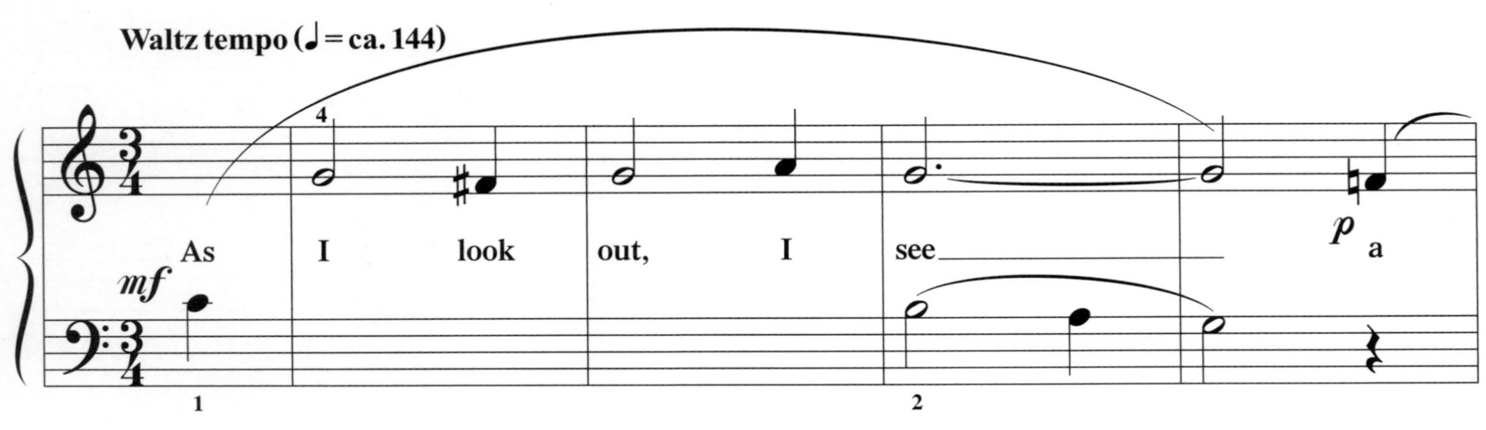

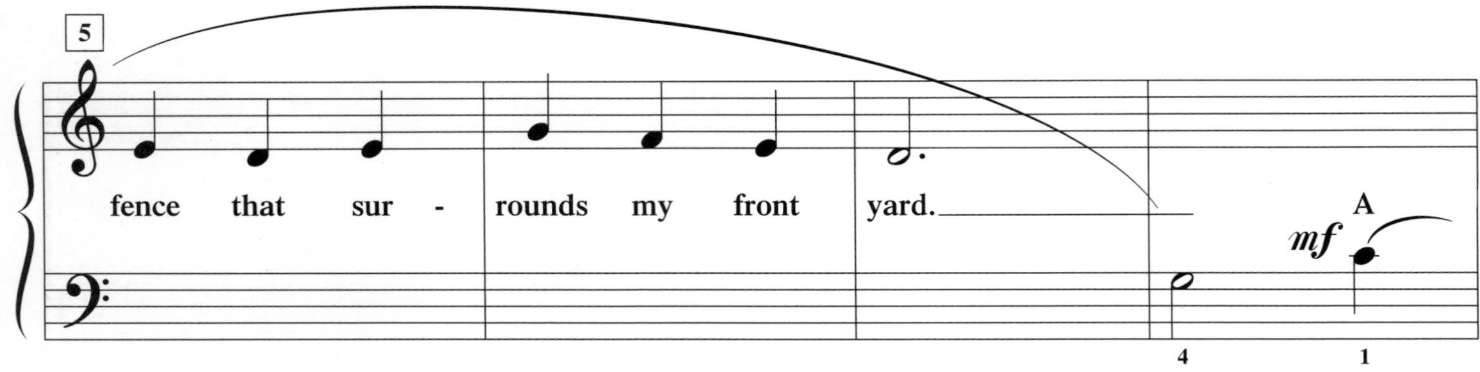

Teacher Duet: (Student plays 1 octave higher)

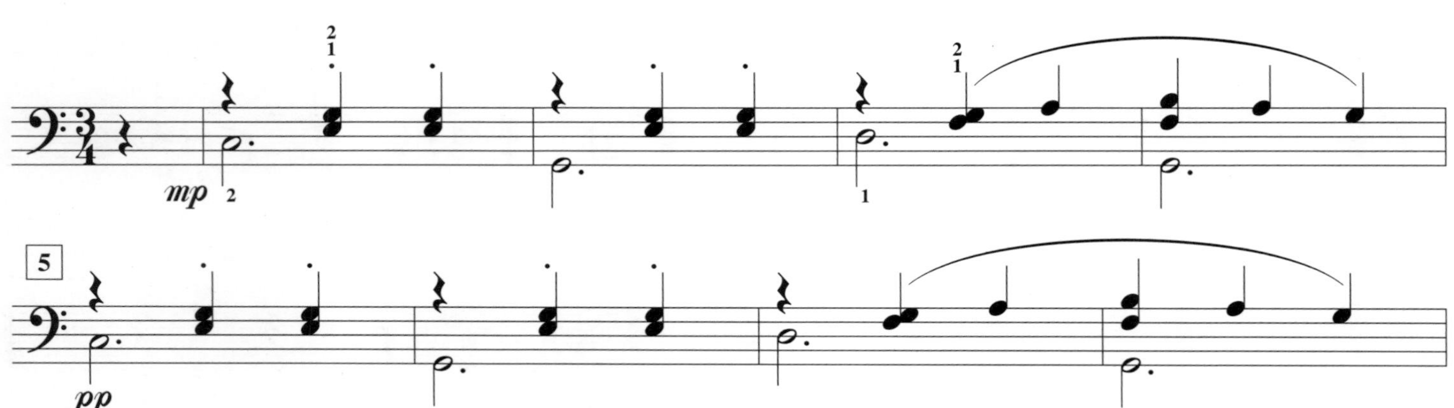

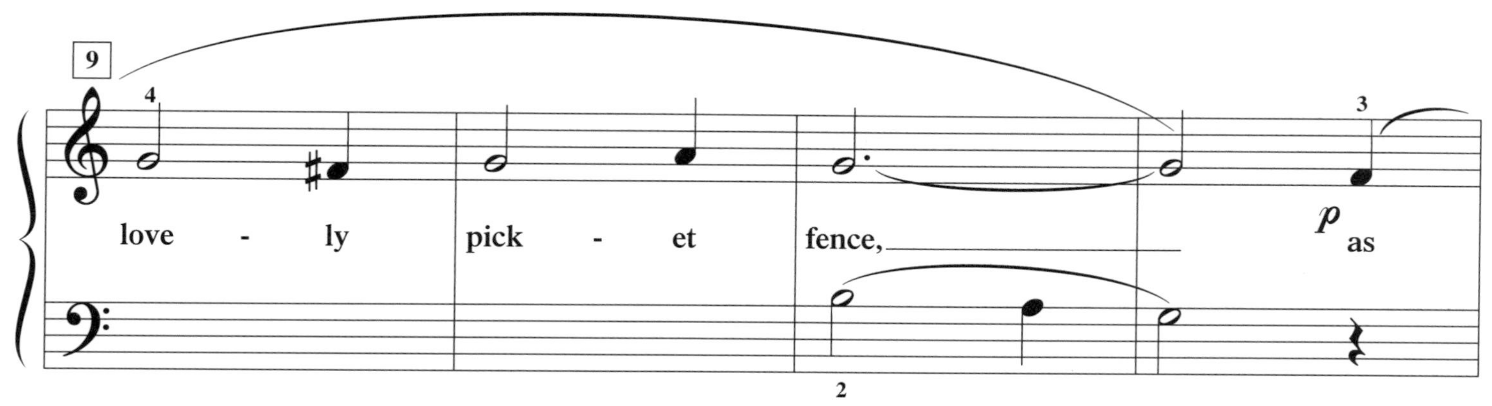
9
love - ly pick - et fence,
p as

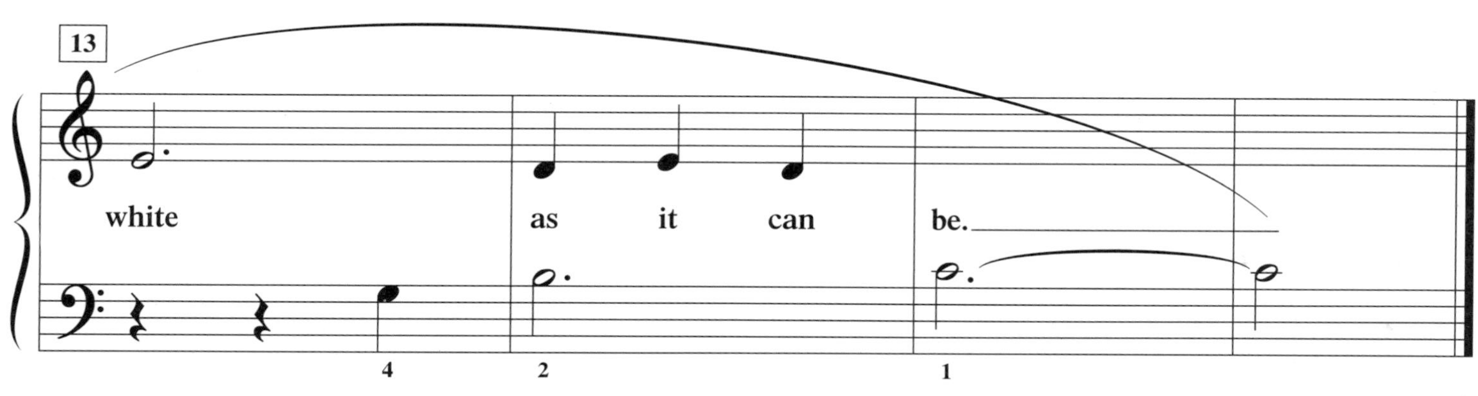
13
white as it can be.

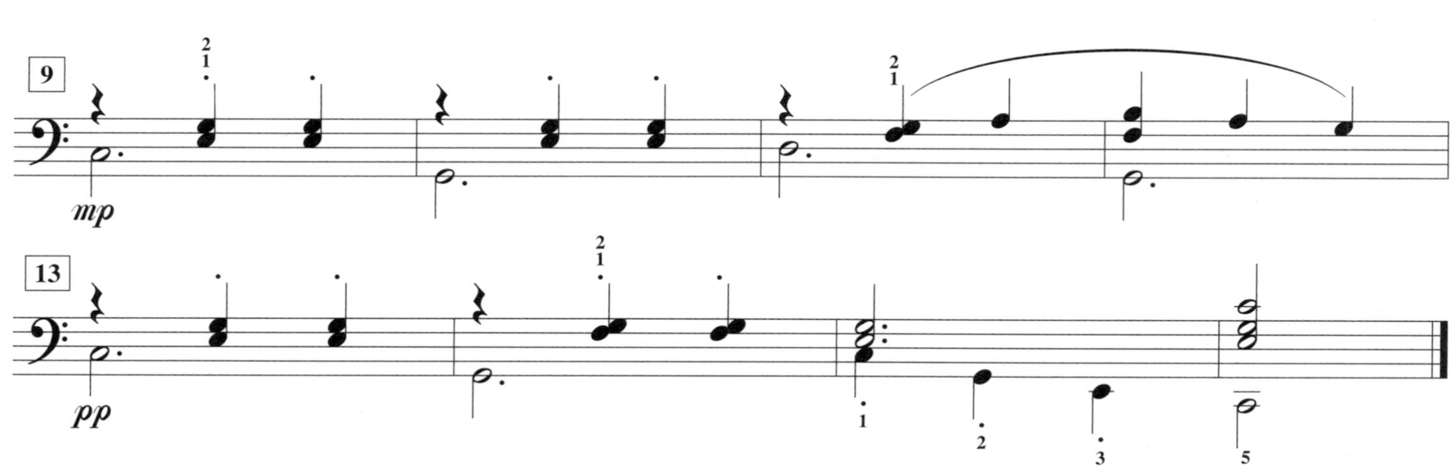
9
mp
13
pp

Squirrels on the Fence

Perkily (♩ = ca. 84)

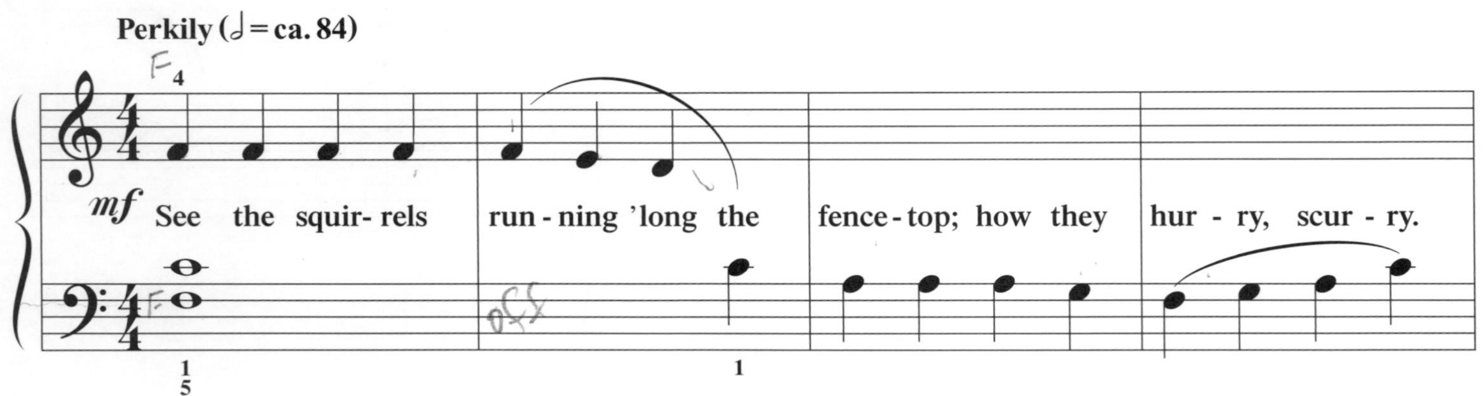

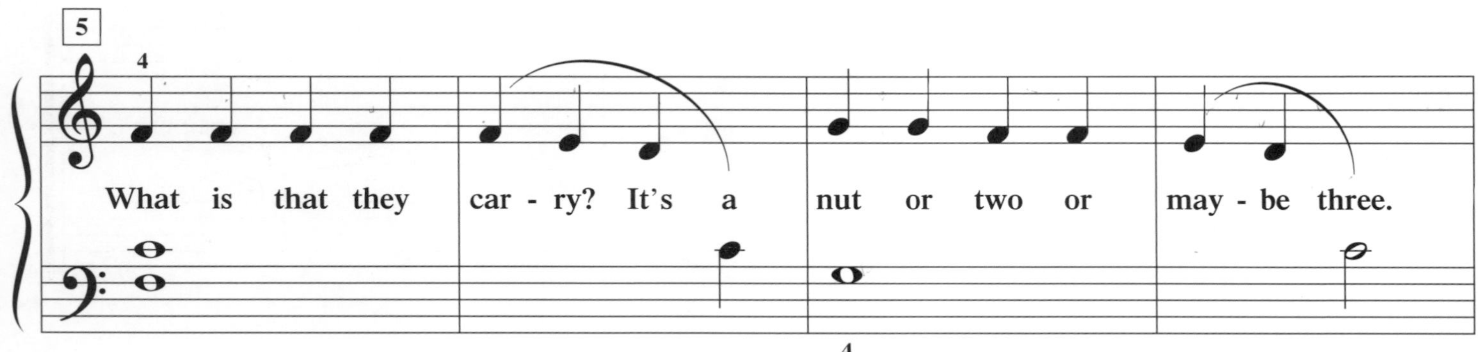

Teacher Duet: (Student plays 1 octave higher)

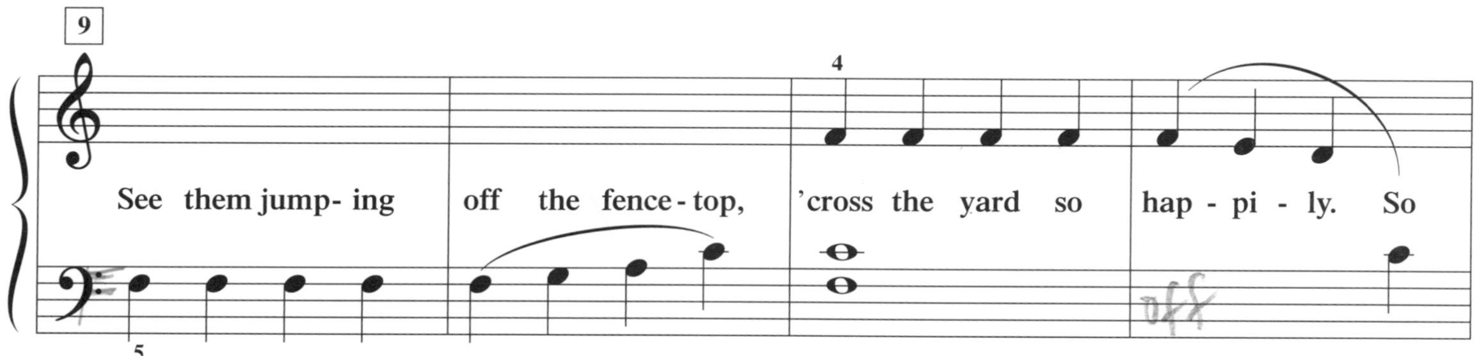
9
4
See them jump- ing
off the fence - top,
'cross the yard so
hap - pi - ly. So
5
off

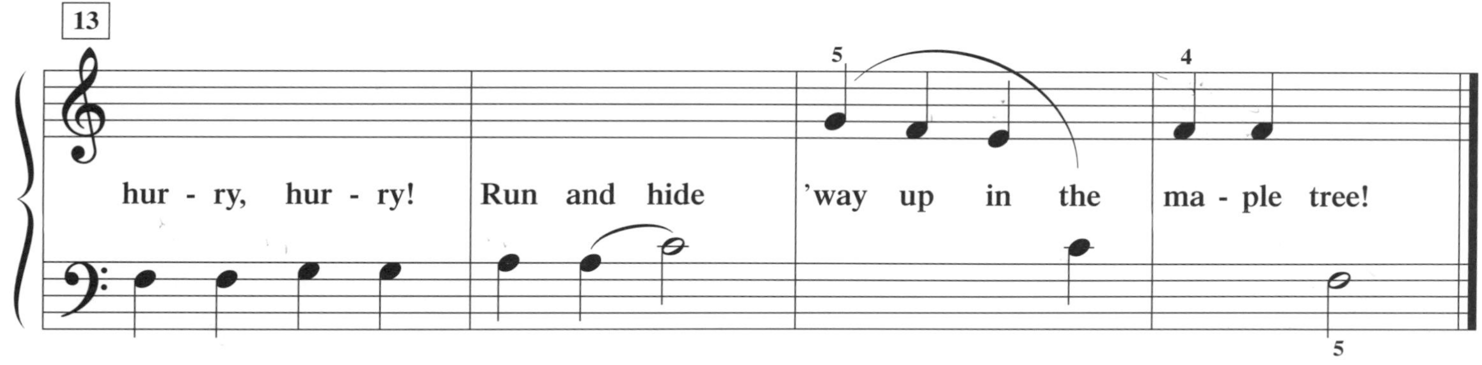
13
5
4
hur - ry, hur - ry!
Run and hide
'way up in the
ma - ple tree!
5

9
13
2
3

Here Comes the Mailman

Happily (𝅗𝅥 = ca. 100)

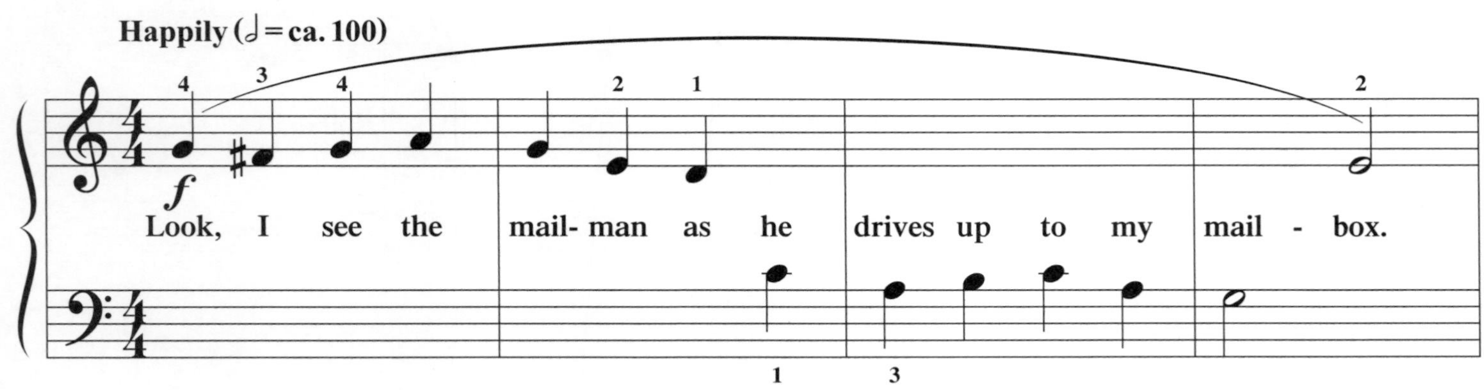

Teacher Duet: (Student plays 1 octave higher)

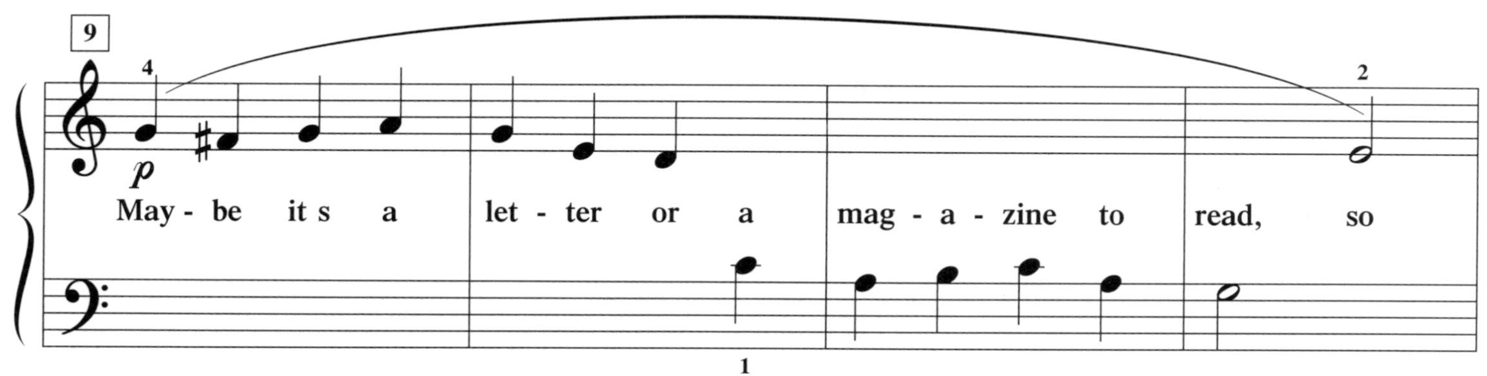
9
4
p
2
May - be it s a let - ter or a mag - a - zine to read, so
1

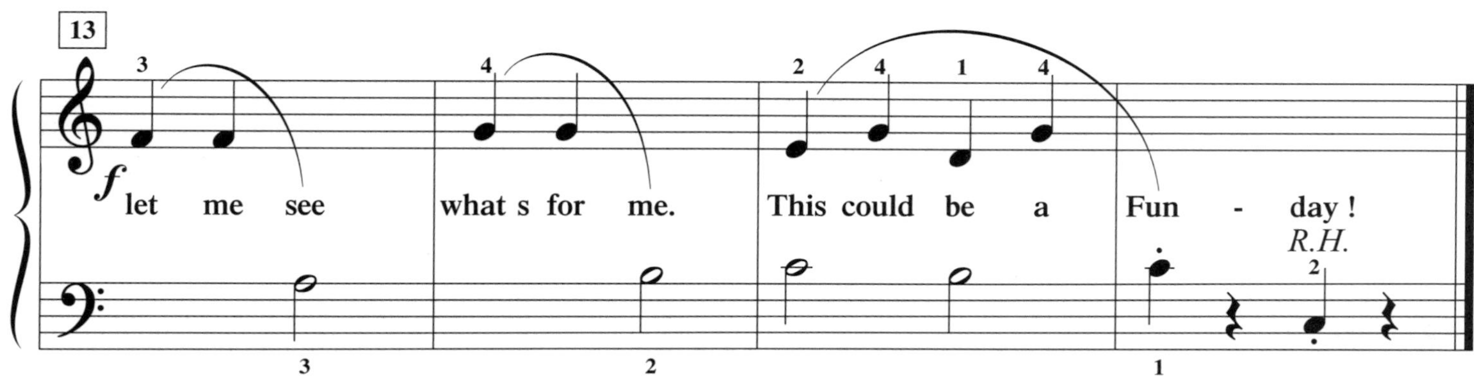
13
3
4
2 4 1 4
f
let me see what s for me. This could be a Fun - day !
R.H.
2
3
2
1

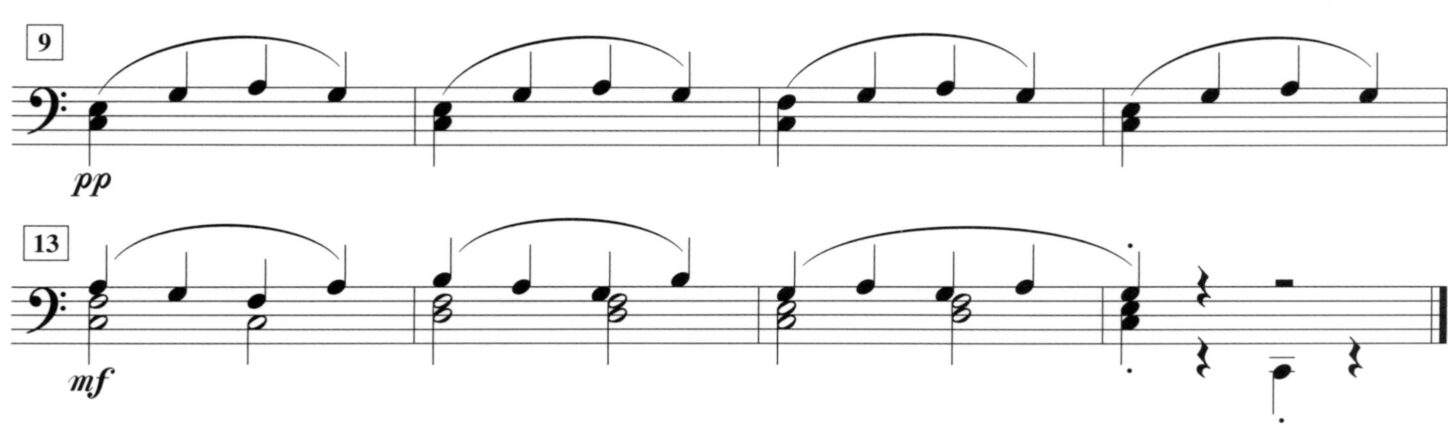
9
pp
13
mf

The Ant Brigade

Briskly (♩= ca. 132)

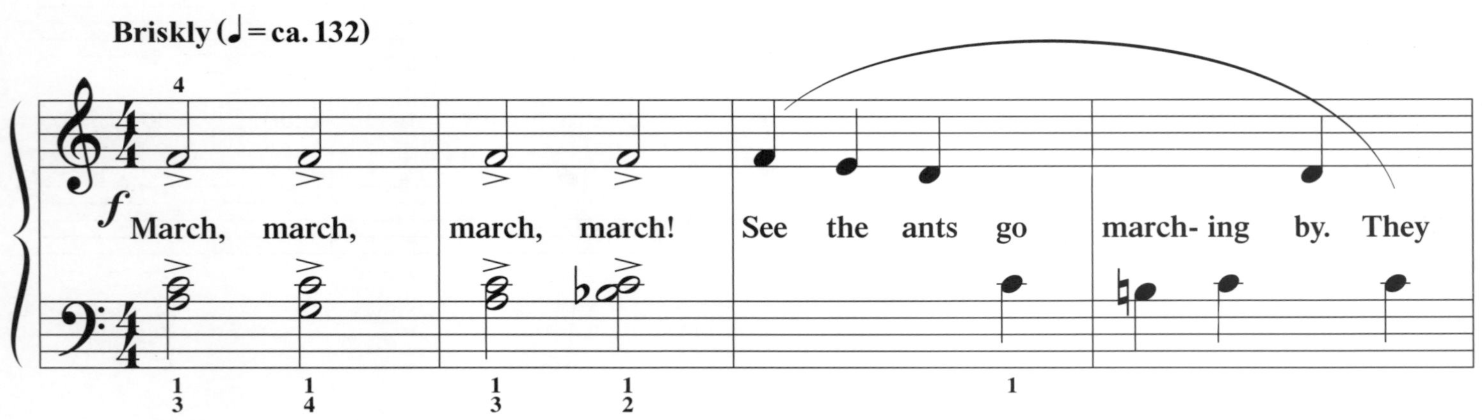

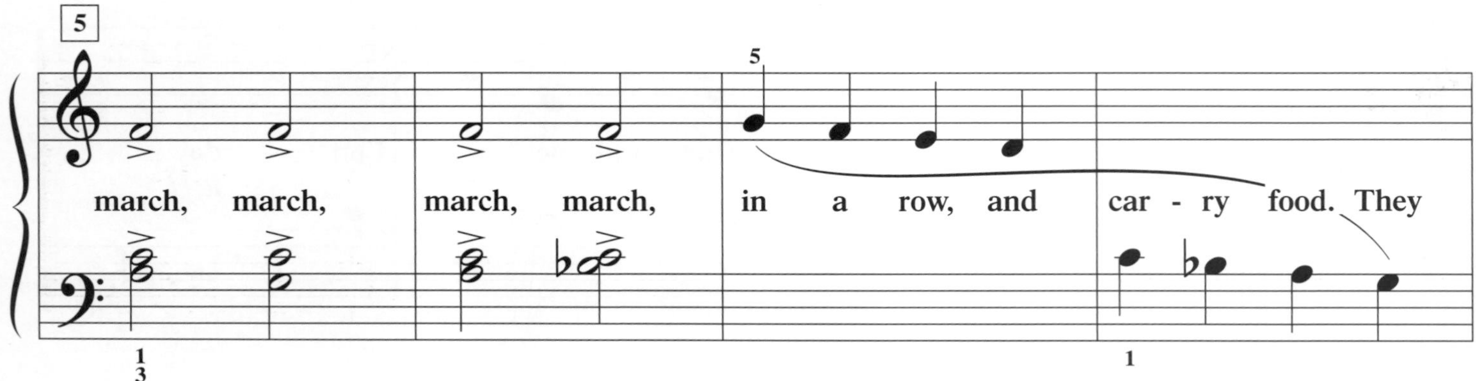

Teacher Duet: (Student plays 1 octave higher)

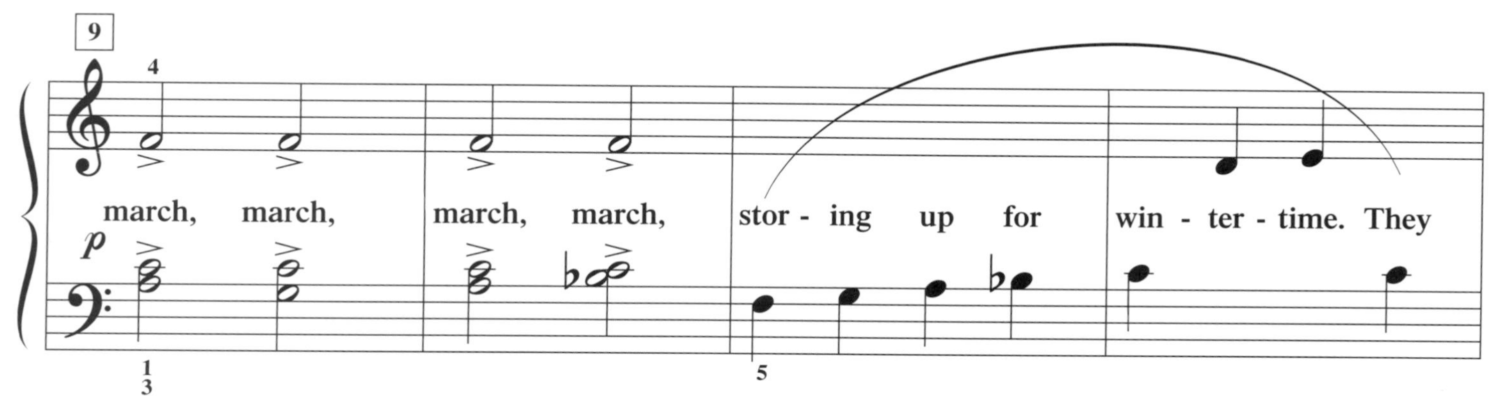
9
4
march, march, march, march, stor - ing up for win - ter - time. They
p
1
3
5

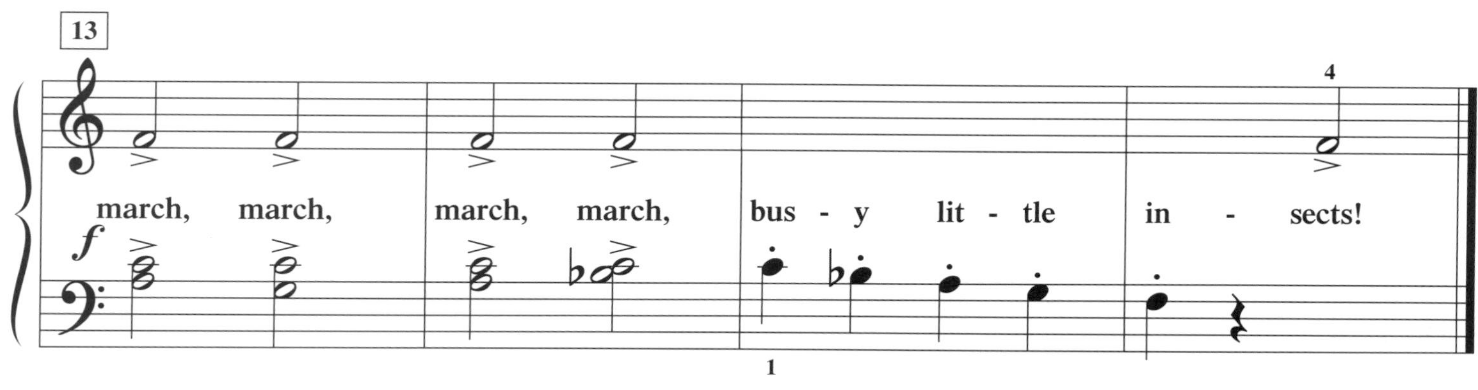
13
4
march, march, march, march, bus - y lit - tle in - sects!
f
1

9
3
pp
13
mf
1
2
5
3
1

A Beautiful Sunset

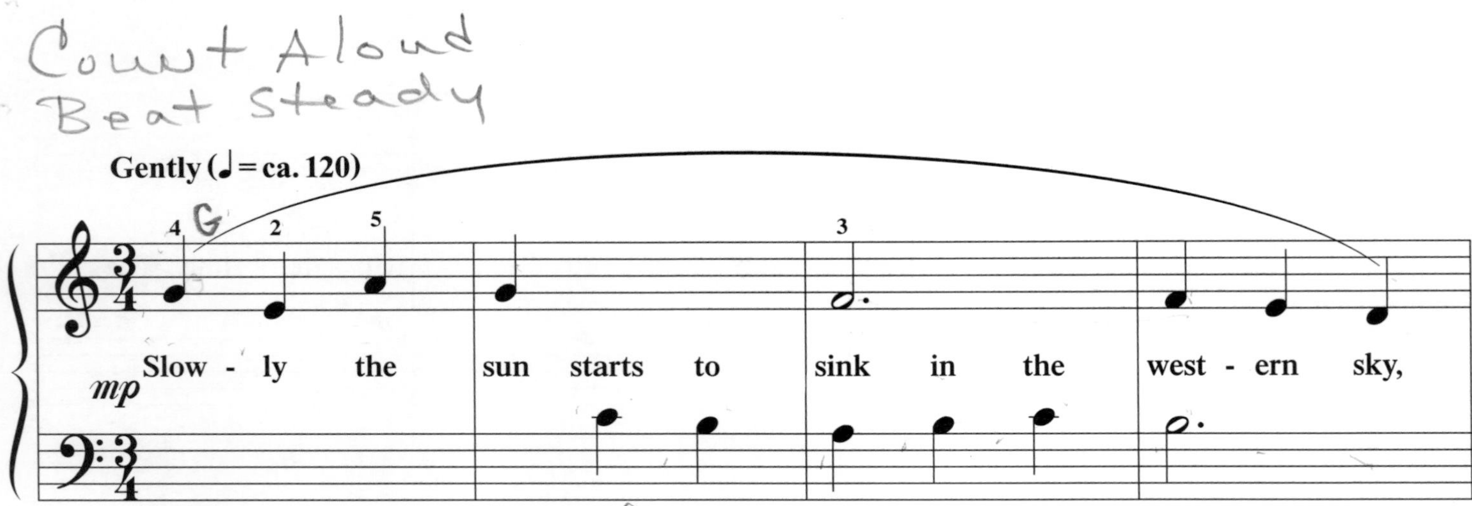

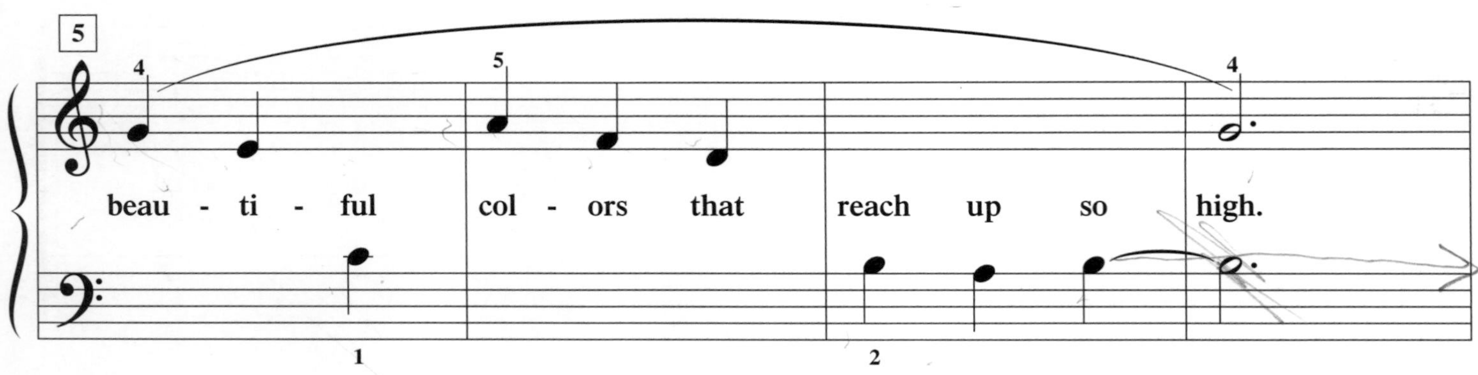

Teacher Duet: (Student plays 1 octave higher)

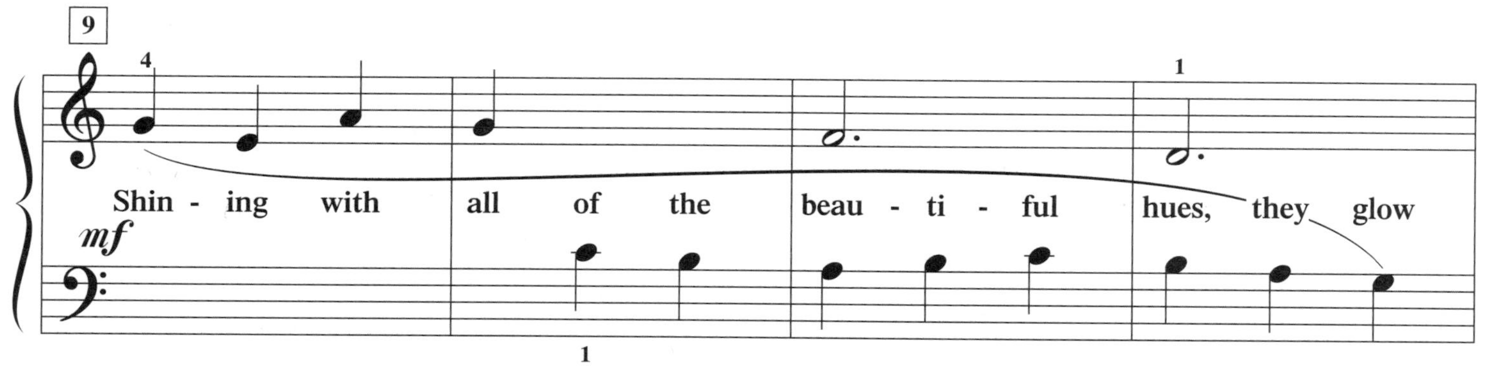
9
Shin - ing with all of the beau - ti - ful hues, they glow
mf

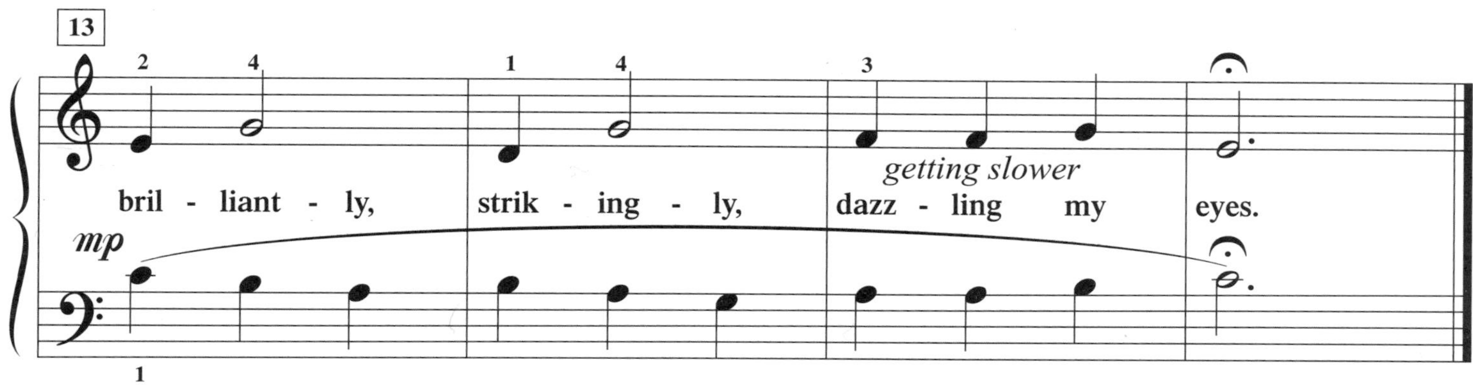
13
getting slower
bril - liant - ly, strik - ing - ly, dazz - ling my eyes.
mp

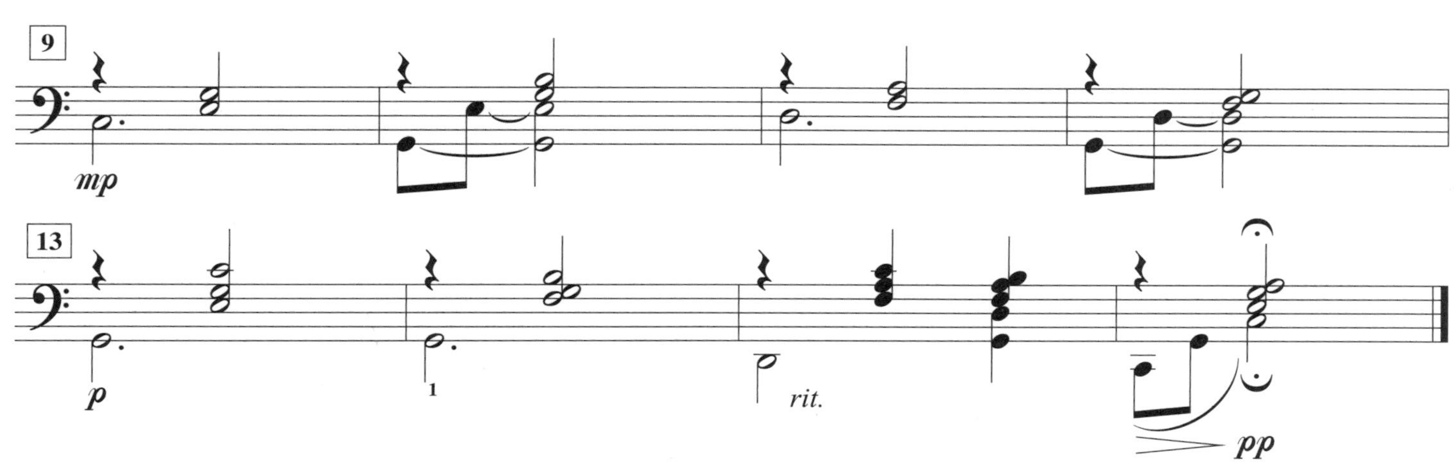
9
mp
13
p
rit.
pp

Clouds Drifting By

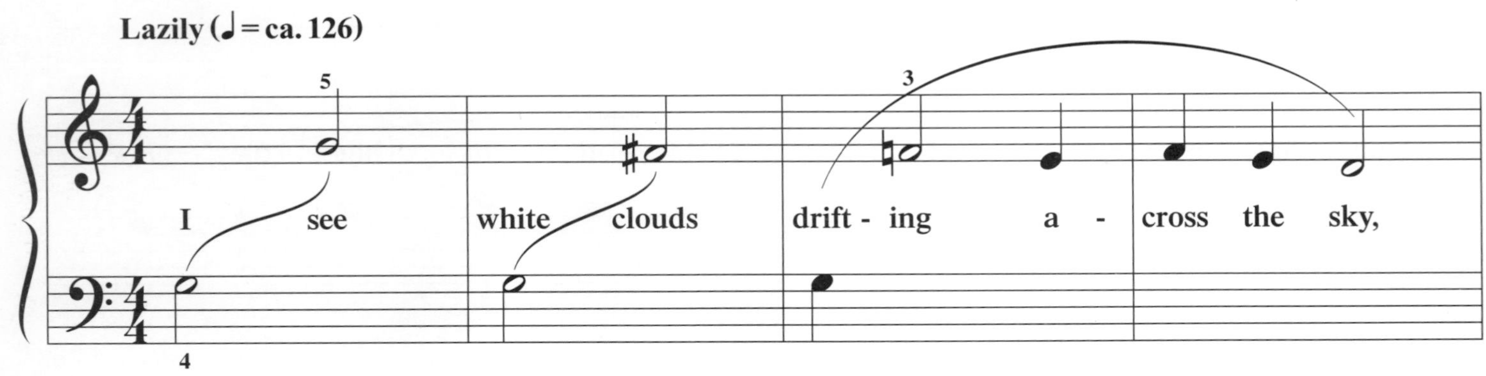

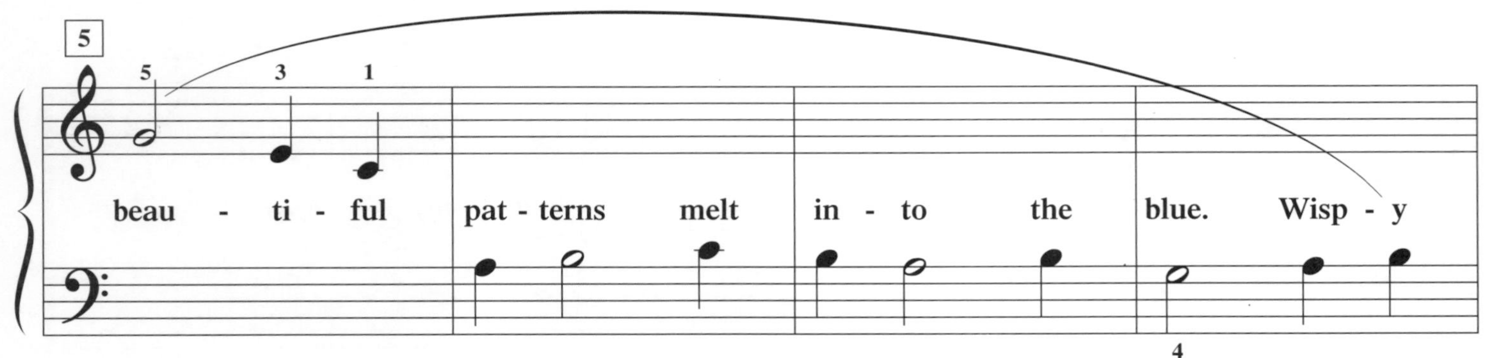

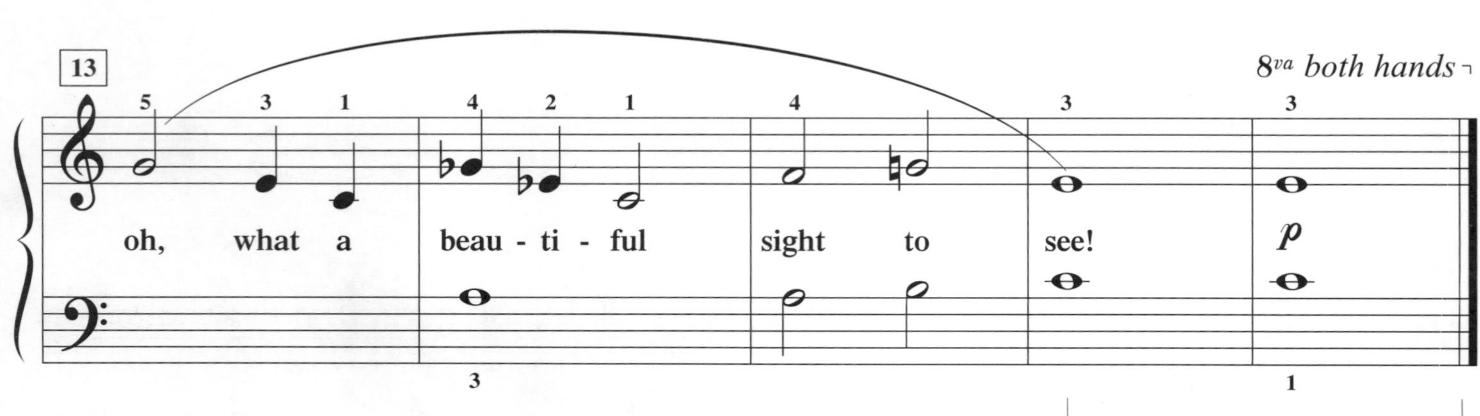